2nd Edition

FALSE PROPHETS

of

FALSE PROFIT$

SECRETS OF HOW FOREIGN NATIONS STOLE
OUR JOBS AND HOW TO TAKE OUR JOBS BACK

BJ Williamson

Lanite Publishing, LLC

Dedication

This book is dedicated to the generations of Americans who worked hard and sacrificed so that their children and grandchildren could have a better life.

God Bless America

Contents

Introduction

Seeing mass layoffs that struck at the heart of Americans compelled me to write this book. I saw people laid off who had worked their way through college and had helped our country become the world's technology leader. I sought answers. Why were Americans being laid off by the thousands in big successful American corporations? Why were young American college graduates unable to find jobs? It was a daunting task. I had to dig through volumes of articles that camouflaged the truth. Then finally I would discover a piece of the hidden puzzle. It was like trying to solve a 3,000 piece puzzle with 10,000 pieces mixed in that didn't belong. Many times I put this project aside overwhelmed at the task. Then I would see more American college graduates who could not find jobs, or another layoff. I would look into people's eyes and see the often unspoken hurt and fear of losing everything they worked so hard to earn. And, I knew this book must be completed. I searched for answers and found some shocking discoveries.

The goal of this book is to help restore the American dream for Americans.

Note: Because of the extensive number of sources reference numbers are provided in [brackets] arranged numerically in a list at the back of the book. Certain words have *italics* and <u>underlining</u> added for emphasis in quotations and/or key points. Because it would be burdensome to readers to repeatedly state: "according to" named source, under document heading, by these authors, on this date" each time a source is mentioned you should read with the understanding that information cited is according to the source.

Chapter 1

Mystery Loss of 15 Million Jobs

Where did our jobs go?

It can be gut-wrenching is you're a college graduate who worked hard, studied, got good grades and have great references, but still you cannot find a job. On top of that, you may owe $20,000-$100,000 and the clock is ticking for you to start making payments. Moving back in to live with your parents was not the reward you expected for earning your degree. You invested in your future so where is your shot at the American dream? You have talent. You want to use your education and skills. Maybe you would like to get married, buy a home and have a family. You need a job.

Or, perhaps you're an American who had a good job. You made a lot of valuable contributions to your company, and yet you were displaced by a foreign worker. When you lost your job you lost your insurance, and then months later you were facing foreclosure. Your family is coming apart. Your kids don't want to go to school or study because they saw what happened to you. Besides, you have no money to pay for their college. Can you restore the American Dream for you and your children? You need a job.

They key to restoring your American Dream is to:

1. Find out where our jobs went.
2. Show how it pays to hire you.
3. Persuade Congress to pass legislation that rewards companies that hire Americans like you.

Where did our Jobs Go?

"The Phantom 15 Million," a 2011 article in the *National Journal*, by Jim Tankersley, reported: "*We certainly didn't see it coming. At the turn of the millennium, the Bureau of Labor Statistics predicted the US economy would create nearly 22 million net new jobs in the 2000s, only slightly fewer than the boom 1990s yielded. The economists predicted "good opportunities for jobs...through 2010."* [972] Instead of adding 22 million jobs we only added 7 million. Where were the additional 15 million jobs?

"*Job growth in the 2000s was the lowest of any decade ever recorded by the federal government, stretching back to the 1940s.*" [972] Tankersley said that technology advancements and international markets paid off for American companies but not for American workers. Economics professors in our top universities were puzzled. They could not understand "*our lost decade of job growth.*" [972]

"*Researchers are just starting to piece together the evidence, and no one can yet finger the culprit.*" Tankersley wrote, "*America's jobs crisis began a decade ago. Long before the housing bubble burst and Wall Street melted down, something in our national job-creation machine went horribly wrong.*" And, he said, "*Even now, no one really knows why.*" [972]

Economists wondered why American companies are sitting on "*nearly $2 trillion in cash*" instead of investing it in "*domestic innovation and the jobs it should create.*"[972] However, labor economist Howard F. Rosen observed: "*US companies are investing in plants and equipment, just not in our borders.*" [972] Then he asks why they are investing overseas instead of at home. Have Americans become less innovative?

Tankersley used the production of iPhones as an example of shipping jobs overseas: "*the iPhone, one of the United States' top innovations of the past decade, actually contributes nearly $2 billion to our trade deficit because it is almost entirely produced and assembled in Asia.*" He wrote that if production was moved to America, "*the company would still turn a 50 percent profit on every one it sold.*" [972]

"The Trillion Dollar Question"

Tankersley asked what we needed to do to fix this. Should we invest more, or should we cut back on foreign trade?

David E. Altig a Federal Reserve Bank VP commented on the mystery behind our massive job losses: "*It's the trillion-dollar question.....something big has happened. I really don't think we have a complete story yet.*" [972]

Some of the puzzling questions leading economists asked:

1) Why "*US job creation had stalled so spectacularly in the past decade*"?

2) Why the US is losing our comparative advantage in college educated brain power?

3) Why our population grew faster than our workforce?

All the economists Tankersley consulted said education was the key. They advised that we needed to encourage Americans to get more educated. They found our younger generation was not better educated than their parents. In contrast, they said the younger generation in developing nations was better educated than their parents. So economists speculated that "*educational stagnation*" may be our problem. Tankersley summed up the economists responses to: "I wish we knew the answer." He said, "*Before we can fix our jobs machine, we must first figure out what broke it.*" [972]

Were young Americans to blame? Let's take a look at some extensive research into our job losses and economic plunges. While it is complicated, if we put together the pieces, maybe we can solve this job loss mystery puzzle and more.

Chapter 2

H-1B Job Heist

Entry level high tech jobs used to go to young Americans graduating from college.

Now many entry level high tech jobs are channeled to visa workers.

One of the biggest secrets kept from the American public is the H-1B visa bill passed by Congress in 1990 that allowed foreigners with a college degree to seek employment in the USA. Shockingly this 3 year "*temporary*" visa program is over 23 years old now!

If you are an American you probably never heard of the H-1B— that is unless you lost your job to one. However, it is very important for you to know about the H-1B visa program and how it has been used to take computer information technology (IT), engineering, and other professional jobs from Americans. [47]

Executives testified to Congress that we had a serious shortage of high tech workers. They said they needed to *temporarily* fill jobs with foreign workers until enough Americans could be educated. Executives assured Congress that they would only hire foreign workers if they could not find qualified Americans. [63]

Our government did not seek an independent source to verify the high tech worker shortage actually existed. Bowing to the pressure from lobbyists, in 1990, under the first Bush administration, Congress passed the H-1B *non-immigrant visa (NIV)* program. The H-1B program allowed executives to *temporarily* fill open high tech jobs for three years with foreign workers. H-1Bs could extend their visas for up to three additional years. After their visas expired H-1Bs were required by law to return to their country of origin.

Executives in Silicon Valley were the prime lobbyists for the controversial H-1B visa program. How did they get Congress to pass the H-1B legislation? They gave money to both our political parties through bipartisan lobbying. Executives used corporate money to "buy" our politicians: "*corporations make political contributions to assure the passage of legislation.*" [63]

Congress did not require businesses hiring H-1Bs to show they attempted to hire Americans first. However, *Congress did require that H-1Bs must be paid the prevailing wage to protect US workers from being replaced by cheaper foreign workers.* This wage requirement shows that Congress suspected the motive was cheaper workers, not a worker shortage.

Another indicator Congress knew something was awry; it set a 65,000 a year H-1B visa quota cap. Imagine 65,000 Americans a year lost their high tech jobs to foreigners through an act of Congress.

It was Fraud 1, 2, and 3 and...

Given the fraud and deceptions that executives used to get H-1B legislation passed, the "transfer" of high tech US citizens' jobs may be viewed as a theft of these jobs.

1) False claims that we had a "*desperate shortage*" of high tech workers. These shortage claims were contradicted by the mass layoffs of American high tech workers.

2) False claims that foreign workers were the "*best and brightest*" and were needed to create a "world class" workforce. This was not credible given the United States' was the world's technology leader.

3) False claims of "*cost savings*" from replacing Americans with foreign workers. The US trade deficit and the Economic Circulation Model you will learn about in this book prove the cost savings claims are false.

It is appalling that if someone steals your wallet you have more legal protection than if they steal your job.

High Tech Worker Shortage Fraud

Several investigations found that the claims of a US high tech worker shortage were false.

Dr. Gene Nelson found that at the time the H-1B bill was passed, we had 13 million people trained in science and engineering and *only ¼ were employed in their field*. Therefore, *we had a high tech job shortage, not a high tech worker shortage*. For every job we had one American working and three American backup replacements trained. He testified before the US House of Representatives in 1999 that the H-1B was harming American workers. Nelson traced the shortage claims back to our National Science Foundation (NSF) which he said made the claims to increase its budget. [47]

In 2000, the *"temporary"* H-1B program was ten years old! Yet, worker shortage claims continued. For example, the Information Technology Association of America (ITAA) claimed that 800,000 computer jobs went unfilled. [289] This was contradicted by our US *Department of Commerce which found no proof that a shortage of American programmers existed, and that an alarming 28% of new programming jobs were going to H-1Bs*. [26] Moreover, Dr. Norman Matloff, a critic of the H-1B, surveyed University of California-Davis computer science graduates and found that *less than half were able to get programming jobs*. [63]

Dr. Matloff criticized the computer industry in December 2000 for hiring public relations (PR) firms to fill US media with claims of severe programmer shortages. Matloff noted that H-1Bs were hired because they were cheaper, not because any shortage existed. Moreover, *he believed that the US Congress had ample evidence that the shortage did not exist*. [26]

The Phyllis Schlafly Report in its June 2003 issue titled: "What the Global Economy Costs Americans" covered the following subtitles: *"The Scam of the H-1B Visas," "The Scam of L-1 Visas," "The Scam of Outsourcing," and "Comments from the Engineers Replaced by Foreigners."* [63]

DUKE PROFESSOR TESTIFIED US HAD NO ENGINEER SHORTAGE

Vivek Wadhwa, an engineering professor at Duke University, testified on May 16, 2006 to the *U.S. House of Representatives Committee on Education and the Workforce* that the US did not have a shortage of engineers. He said 30-40% of engineering graduates with Masters degrees took jobs outside their profession.

He also told Congress that the 2004 reports claiming China produced 600,000 engineers, India 350,000 and the United States only 70,000 were flawed. He said the Chinese Ministry of Education and India's NASCOMM inflated their numbers by counting people who only had certificates.

Wadhwa warned against the US graduating more American citizen engineers *saying it could cost the US our competitive edge, because it would reduce salaries and cause unemployment.* Surprisingly, he asked: *"If a certain type of engineering job can be done more cost effectively in India or China, why should we invest in graduating more of those types of engineers?"* [779] This is bad advice. Because of the wage gap just about any job can be done cheaper in India or China–including his job. We should not give up control of engineering to India or China.

When Wadhwa testified, did the Committee know that he was one of the first CEO's to hire H-1Bs, and that he said he hired H-1Bs because they were cheaper? [780]

Less than a year after his testimony, in January 2007, Wadhwa wrote an article "Open Doors Wider for Skilled Immigrants." He advocated bringing in more foreign programmers and engineers even though he was well aware that this threatened our nation's "competitive edge" by reducing salaries and causing high unemployment. [687] His article appears to contradict his testimony where he advised Congress that we did not need more American engineers.

"Best and Brightest" Fraud

After their shortage claims were debunked, sponsors then argued H-1Bs were the "best and brightest." For instance, "The Indians of Silicon Valley," a *Fortune* article in 2000, said American engineers *"typically aren't as talented as those from India."* [289] They tried to equate graduate school degrees to the *"best and brightest"* to justify preferential hiring of H-1Bs. [49] However, multiple investigations found the H-1B *"best and brightest"* claims were false.

H-1Bs were supposed to have college degrees and special skills. However, the US consular office in India found that 21% of the H-1B applications had fraudulent information, plus an additional 29% were suspected of being fraudulent. This meant that *up to 50% of the H-1B visas granted in India may have been gotten through fraud.* [34] [302]

Senator Dianne Feinstein in 1998 said that <u>85% of H-1Bs took entry level jobs that should go to young Americans graduating from college</u>. She found H-1Bs were not paid as exceptional skills workers, but rather were often paid less than prevailing wages as required by law. [15] [12]

An INS audit in 2000 also discovered that many H-1Bs used fake credentials. That year, foreign born computer programmers received less than 8% (9 out of 115) of the Electrical and Electronic Engineers awards, while *Americans earned over 92% of the awards.* [44] This was ten years into the H-1B when 25% of the scientists and engineers working in Silicon Valley were foreign born. [372] [272] If they were the "best and brightest" they should have received more than 25%.

Back to Wadhwa's 2006 testimony to the workforce committee trying to decide if we needed to invest to educate more American engineers to keep ahead of India and China. In an endeavor to convince them this was not necessary, Wadhwa testified that: *"all available data indicates that the <u>vast majority of Indian and Chinese graduates are not close to the standards of US graduates</u>."* And he reported that IIT (*India's Indian Institute of Technology*) graduates who came to Duke to study were *"<u>only as good as the average American student</u>."* [779]

H-1Bs Linked to Layoffs

Dr. Matloff reported in 2003 that executives in several major corporations admitted that they had misused H-1B and L1 visa workers to displace American workers. He *proposed several reforms including a required 6 month waiting period before hiring H-1Bs after a layoff.* [329] Outsourcing lobbies repeatedly blocked any attempts to reform or end the H-1B program.

Companies were laying off Americans and hiring H-1Bs. Oracle, Cisco Systems, Intel and Sun Microsystems in Silicon Valley were in a list of companies hiring the most H-1Bs in 2000. The following year these same companies did massive layoffs of US citizens.

Many H-1Bs who lost their jobs in the 2000 dotcom crash stayed in the US illegally. Of course, they were not filling a US worker shortage. They were competing against Americans for hard to find high tech jobs. Our government failed to deport visa violators.

Moreover, *our government granted over 715,000 work visas and permitted 110,000 foreigners on visitor visas to work in the US in 2001 in the midst of a recession!* [74] "H-1B Visa Demand Rises," a 2002, *AsianWeek.com* story said the INS could not produce a count of the number of H-1B applications filed by US companies laying off Americans. [40]

The president of the *Institute of Electrical and Electronics Engineers (IEEE)* told the Senate in 2003 that companies misused the H-1B. He said that companies used these visas to try-out foreign workers including *illegal aliens, foreign students and foreigners with visitor visas.* [54]

The IEEE reported that *during a time when over 500,000 high tech jobs were cut, almost 800,000 new or renewal H-1B visas were issued!* It requested an investigation of H-1B and L-1B hiring practices. *Not only that,* in 2001 if found 329,000 L-1 visa workers in the US. *H-1B and L-1 visas were used to fill jobs that Americans needed and were qualified to fill.* [62] The INS and the US Department of Labor initiated investigations into H-1B visa fraud by some of our biggest American high tech companies. [34]

Congress Protected Visa Workers but Not Americans

Although the H-1B was approved by Congress as a *non-immigrant visa (NIV)*, most applicants planned from the beginning to stay in the US. They sought green cards. Therefore, the H-1B visas not only rob US citizens of current job opportunities, these visas had long term and permanent negative impact on the high tech job market for Americans. [397] Moreover, *the H-1B foreign workers in our country opened to door to offshore our professional jobs to foreign workers in other countries.*

Shockingly, Congress made it illegal to favor US citizens over H-1Bs during a layoff. [31] This is unconscionable given that the H-1B was only granted as a temporary visa to fill jobs where there was a "shortage" of Americans. The Senate also unanimously approved an amendment that provided protection to foreign workers who filed complaints against the H-1B visa program. [14] So we were taxed to award money to H-1B workers who took our jobs.

In contrast, our Congress failed to protect US citizens who lost their jobs due to H-1B fraud. Executives became adept at modifying job requirements to favor hiring H-1Bs. Much of the hiring was done in secret. They did not even have to post the jobs so Americans could apply. [49] It was so blatant that some executives hired H-1Bs first, and then wrote the job requirements. [468] Some job search sites such as *hotjobs.com*, and *monster.com* had their listings filled with ads recruiting H-1Bs. [144]

Often, talented well-educated highly skilled Americans were displaced by lesser skilled *H-1Bs who only had a couple of Java programming classes.* [24] On top of that many H-1Bs, who did have the US education credentials claimed, may have obtained their degree through fraudulent college applications as you will see when you read more.

So what we have here are layers of carefully crafted fraud to deny young college-educate Americans entry level jobs in their field of study. And, to displace college-educated American workers who made our country the technology leader with foreign workers.

Rajat Gupta–Outsourcing & Guilty Insider Trading!

"Offshoring work will spur innovation, job creation, and dramatic increases in productivity that will be passed on to the (American) consumer," Rajat Gupta claimed in a 2003 *BusinessWeek* story, "The Rise of India." [300] Gupta, an immigrant from India, was Managing Director of McKinsey & Co. one of the largest management consulting firms in the world. [334] [187] He advised American CEOs to cut costs by replacing American engineers paid $80,000 a year with engineers in India who cost only $10,000. [300] McKinsey & Co also advised in 2004 that offshoring our service jobs would cut costs by 45% to 55%; and that *huge profits would result since 14 million US service jobs could be offshored!* [6]

Were US clients told that McKinsey employed many consultants in India who had a vested interest in forecasting profits from offshoring to India? Critics of McKinsey said the company operates in secrecy making it difficult to scrutinize its performance. [696] Enron was headed by McKinsey alumni; and, Enron was one of McKinsey's biggest clients when it collapsed. [696]

*Gupta referred to outsourcing as a **"revolution"** and asserted that only 3% of the jobs that could be outsourced had been outsourced in* a 2007 interview on the PBS show, "Foreign Exchange with Fareed Zakaria." Gupta told how he had used consulting to persuade US companies to *offshore our research jobs to India as early as 1992. Zakaria asked if America had only seen the "tip of the iceberg with outsourcing?" And Gupta responded, "Yeah."* [640]

Gupta had nearly $100 million by 2012, when he was found guilty of insider trading. As a member of the board of directors of Goldman Sachs, he was caught leaking information to a hedge fund billionaire who purchased $43 million of Goldman stock. Columbia Law Professor John Coffee said, *"Symbolically, you can't get a more egregious case. It is like catching a Supreme Court justice leaking the results of a decision breaking up IBM."* [1066] How much of Gupta's $100 million come from outsourcing and offshoring US jobs to India? Was his outsourcing *"revolution"* of sending our jobs to India *"economic espionage to benefit a foreign country?"* [576] *If so, was this a bigger crime than his securities fraud?*

Is The H-1B the Biggest Scam in History?

Investigating our job losses was like the time I found a small soft spot on our deck railing. Using a screwdriver to take out what looked like a shallow spot the size of a pencil eraser; I was quite surprised when the tool sunk in about an inch deep. And when I pulled the tool out a big chunk of rotten wood broke off. That 2 by 6 on the surface still looked good and solid and was stained a nice cedar brown. However, water had seeped into a long thin crack and had been rotting the board for some time without being noticed. The board was ruined and had to be replaced. I soon found two more boards that had to be replaced.

When I began investigating our job losses I thought it was a small local problem. Never did I imagine what I began to uncover. Researching I would dig in and then much to my surprise I would discover a big rotten chunk much worse than I expected. One discovery would lead me to the next. The scope of what I found is mindboggling.

I found the H-1B job heist was the lever used by foreign nations to turn our economy on end. It is the underlying reason why our nation is teetering on the brink economically. Since its inception in 1990 has the H-1B program been the biggest scam in history?

Chapter 3

American Job Losses

What happened to: "Our employees are our most valuable resource."

The new mantra is train your foreign replacement—you've been outsourced.

If you are an American, you or someone you know, has probably lost their job to a foreign worker. Among the first casualties were American textile workers and manufacturing assembly workers. Our Government and Corporate America reassured us that we would keep the higher paying knowledge-based jobs. They claimed the key to job security was to earn a college degree.

However, the truth is American jobs targeted by foreign nations went well beyond our manufacturing jobs, and the lower skilled jobs such as call centers, customer service, and back office. *Foreign H-1B visa workers went after our high tech jobs, media jobs, accounting jobs, legal jobs, medical jobs, consulting jobs and more.* These are many of America's best jobs, jobs of affluence, and jobs of power. [81]

"The answer is education and training," John McCain told Americans in need of jobs. *He blamed Americans for "our inability to adjust to a new world economy,"* and said future jobs are part of *"the information technology revolution."* [690] As a US Senator, he should have known that as a result of H-1B visa legislation passed by Congress, college educated American information technology (IT) workers lost their jobs in droves to foreign H-1B visa workers. This *"temporary" three year foreign worker program was 18 years old at the time of his 2008 campaign.*

College Educated Unemployment Worst in History

President Bush traveled to India in 2007 and gave assurances visa programs and offshoring targeting our professional jobs would continue. He said that *Americans just need to get educated*. [505]

Recall that all the economists consulted about the 15 million US job losses said education was the key. A cursory overview of unemployed Americans quickly debunks the *"educational stagnation"* theory as the cause of our job losses. For example, US Department of Labor reports showed that from 2000-2003 unemployment for college educated Americans increased 95%, and was worse than unemployment for high school dropouts. *The long term unemployment for Americans with college degrees increased 300%!* [140]

It got worse year after year. We were making history–and it was not good. After reviewing Bureau of Labor Statistics in June 2011, The Economic Policy Institute found: "*The class of 2011 will likely face the highest unemployment rate for college graduates...in history.*" More than 1.7 million were graduating with 4 year degrees but job prospects were grim. [970]

Our Job Losses Were Predicted Years in Advance

Our government had ample warnings and opportunities to stop our professional job losses. For example consider these job loss predictions made in 2004:

- *The federal Bureau of Labor Statistics cut US IT job growth predictions through 2012 by 70%. Instead of adding 152,000 IT jobs per year it estimated only 10,600 IT jobs would be added because of offshoring.* [140]

- *Gartner estimated one in four US high tech workers would lose their job to offshore outsourcing to countries such as India by 2010.* [129]

- *Forester Research estimated that 3.3 million professional US jobs with combined wages over $136 billion will be moved offshore by 2015.* [88]

In 2005, one university study calculated that *14 million American white collar jobs were at risk of being sent overseas*. [81]

Decade of Historic Job Losses

The 2000 dotcom crash recession officially ended in June 2001. Historically three out of four people who lost jobs reclaimed them during a recovery. But *this time only two out of four jobs were recovered, and half of the recovered jobs were part time.* [80] From 2001 to 2006 US *communications equipment jobs plummeted 43%, semiconductor & electronic components jobs plummeted 37%, computers and electronic products jobs plummeted by 30%.* [504] What happened?

- US executives *laid off over a million Americans* while applying for H-1Bs in 2001. [362] [40] Foreigners got 991,000 visas to work in the US. [397] *H-1Bs took 9 out of every 10 new computer jobs.* [143]

- US labor experts warned in 2002 that offshore outsourcing was causing vast numbers of high tech job losses that no one was tracking. [105] Our Fortune 500 companies had doubled the number of jobs they offshored in 3 years. [51]

- 70% of laid off American high tech workers in 2003 had used up their unemployment benefits and were unable to find jobs. [143] The unemployment rates for engineering, computer science, and information technology (IT) jobs were the highest in our nation's history. [88]

- The US Department of Labor found in 2004 that 1/3 of the Americans displaced by foreign workers had been unable to find jobs. If they found a job their pay was usually less than half their previous salaries. [81]

- "Offshoring. Outsourcing. Out of Work." in 2005 reported a 35% drop in American engineering jobs. [615]

- The number of "legal" and illegal immigrants flooding into the US in 2006 exceeded the number of jobs created by 500,000. [504] This answers why our population grew faster than our workforce.

- Despite spending record amounts on high tech research, in 2009, high tech job cuts hit the highest level in four years. [966] In April 2009, jobless claims jumped to 669,000 the worst in 26 years. [732]

New jobs in our corporations were going to foreign visa workers in the United States and to offshore foreign workers.

Discriminating against American Workers

While the H-1B caused millions of college educated Americans to lose their jobs, the Americans hurt the most were young Americans. *The H-1B pitted 22 year old Americans graduating with bachelor degrees against 27-30 year old foreign students graduating with Masters degrees or PhDs for entry level US jobs.*

How did we lose so many jobs? Foreign visa workers targeted our advanced technology jobs. They persuaded executives to hire them and lay off Americans by working below market rates. [187]

For example: "Lawsuit Slams Sun's 'Bias' for Indian H-1B Workers," a 2003 article claimed Sun favored hiring H-1B foreign visa workers over Americans. People of India ancestry comprised only 4% of the population in Santa Clara County where Sun Microsystems was headquartered, yet they held 30% or more of the jobs in some of Sun's departments in Santa Clara County. [55]

Outsourcing used to cloak discriminating against Americans:

- *In 2000, an American company replaced a Senior IT executive with an H-1B who then fired the American programmers and outsourced the work to Tata Consultancy, an India outsourcing company that employed H-1Bs in the US.* [28]

- *In 2001, Bank of America outsourced its Human Resources (HR) management to Exult which agreed to hire Bank of America's HR employees. However, Exult then outsourced to HCL and Hexaware. These H-1B "bodyshops," laid off the Americans and forced them to train H-1Bs to get severance pay.* [37]

- *Cigna insurance outsourced its high tech jobs to Satyam, an India outsourcing company.* [63]

According to a 2009 *USAToday* article, *"Jobless Rate at 11.2% for Veterans of Iraq, Afghanistan."* One young veteran looking for a job was told that *"some employers consider a military record almost like having "a felony.""* [743] Denying veterans jobs is disgraceful.

Early Retirement Plans Used to Displace Americans

Isn't age discrimination illegal? To avoid unwanted publicity from layoffs, and to keep the transfer of our jobs to foreign workers out of the limelight, companies pressured Americans over 50 years old to take early retirement. For example, a 2011 USA Today article, 'Why the Jobs are Going Over There," said that in 2005 Cisco began pushing early retirement and *"added twice as many jobs abroad as in the U.S."* [923] The article had the audacity to claim we needed to bring in more visa workers to slow down offshoring of our jobs. This was outrageous because H-1B workers were used as the conduit for offshoring our jobs in the first place. What we need are jobs for young Americans so that they can afford to get married and have children.

Americans Tried to Fight Back

The epicenter of these job losses was in Silicon Valley the heart of our high tech industry. The job losses ripped across our whole country.

Layoffs went well beyond technology companies. They hit accounting firms, law firms, media jobs, and even our banks. For example, Bank of America employees displaced by foreign workers claimed that they were required to sign severance agreements that would cut off their severance pay if they talked to the media. [90]

Executives doing the layoffs used corporate money to pay lawyers to draft severance agreements that forced Americans to train foreigners taking their jobs.

Meanwhile, Americans tried to fight back. But, that's awfully hard to do when you lose your job and have no money to pay expensive lawyers. Laid of Americans needed their severance pay to buy food and cover bills while they searched for jobs.

American Workers & Their Children Devastated

Americans who made our nation the world's technology leader were demeaned and forced to train their foreign replacements to get severance pay. Job losses caused health problems, broken homes; despair... Laid off Americans were left to fend for themselves with little hope of regaining their quality of life and security. [49]

American families were devastated by job losses. In a 2006 *Electronic Engineering Times* outsourcing survey an American said: "*It has forced me into bankruptcy and destroyed my family.*" [528] The survey found that engineers in India took American engineers' jobs because *they were paid $38,300 a year less; however, once they had the jobs they were "anxious for better pay.*" [529] It was the old predatory pricing strategy.

When parents lose their jobs, American children not only lose the money needed to pay for college, they lose the belief that a high tech degree will provide them with employment. A *USAToday* 2009 article, "24 Million Go From 'Thriving' to 'Struggling'," said the American belief that, "*those who work hard and play by the rules can get ahead, and that the next generation will have a better life,*" was being lost. [733]

Mass layoffs forced hardworking well-educated Americans into bankruptcy. In turn, layoffs harmed US businesses where laid off Americans owed money. [143] Hit particularly hard was our housing industry:

- *One survey found that 35% of the households in Silicon Valley had one or more people who lost their job and were unemployed for over three months between 2001 and 2002.* [73]

- *By June 2003, home foreclosures and bankruptcies in the US reached record levels. Almost 1 out of every 100 homes at that time was in foreclosure.* [143]

- *By 2008, one in 54 homes received a foreclosure filing.*

- *From 2007 to 2011 almost 2 million Americans homes were lost to foreclosure each year. That's 8 million American families!* [1039]

Social Contract Broken

It is self destructive for a nation to harm its own citizens, and to favor workers from other countries. Our government and business leaders broke the important social contract that inspired Americans to invent. [122]

One American engineer summed it up: *"When a young American decides to enter the EE profession, he makes a well-understood bargain with society."* If he invests in an education and works hard, he can expect financial rewards and job security. Instead, he said the American engineer had to, *"watch from the sidelines while some stranger benefits from the very infrastructure he spent his life building."* [566]

Another engineer wrote, *"I didn't create jobs out of technology so that they could be moved overseas. I created jobs so that Americans like myself could support their families."* [461]

What Can You Do?

The entire premise of the H-1B program was contrived. It took two years to educate a foreign student in a US graduate school to become qualified to fill an H-1B visa job. Logically an American could have been trained in the same time period. Moreover, how could Congress justify granting up to six years when an American could have been trained in two years or less? [63]

Write to Congress and let them know there are enough college educated Americans to fill all our jobs. Tell them the "educational stagnation" theory is nonsense. If your parents had a college degree and you got a college degree, you did not stagnate.

This chapter was to help you see the scope of the damage caused by the H-1B visa. Now, I will help you discover how this was kept hidden.

Chapter 4

US Media Manipulation

"To bury the truth, buy the media." (Unknown)

Our media was eerily silent while 50% or more of young American college graduates across our country cannot find jobs. And, while well-educated hardworking Americans lost vital high tech jobs, health insurance, homes, their children's' college funds, and more. [972]

Where were the media stories to inform Americans? Where was the empathy for innocent American children whose families were torn apart by job losses? Where was the empathy for young Americans graduating from college burdened with debt and facing a dismal job market?

In 1998, the H-1B "temporary" visa program turned 8 years old! A Harris Poll found that *86% of Americans had little or no knowledge of the H-1B*. When Americans were made aware of the H-1B they were 82% opposed. [36]

By 2003 the H-1B visa program was thirteen years old. The Phyllis Schlafly Report, "What the Global Economy Costs Americans," noted: *"The national media treat H-1B as a non-issue ..."* [63]

When the H-1B program turned 17 years old, an *itbusinessedge.com* article wrote: *"One of the most shocking things about the H-1B program is how little anyone appears to know about it."* [661]

This H-1B is over 23 years old! Still many Americans don't know about this legislation devastating American workers.

60 Minutes Exposed H-1B Fraud in 1993

Before our media was compromised, in October 1993, a *60 Minutes* segment by Leslie Stahl: "North of the Border" did an excellent report exposing that the 3 year old H-1B program was based on fraud. Stahl said executives who displaced Americans with visa workers refused to be interviewed.

She told how "*thousands of unemployed American programmers turn up at every computer job fair in Silicon Valley, and most of them leave disappointed.*" [568] *Why? Companies were not willing to hire an American when they could hire two or more H-1B visa workers for the same price.* Stahl said even small businesses abused the visa to bring in cheap foreign programmers.

Stahl pointed out H-1Bs did not fill a labor shortage, nor did they *have unique talent and skills—a prerequisite for obtaining their visas.* She scoffed at a *six year temporary classification: "That's a joke. Everyone's going to laugh."* [568] And, the *"biggest joke of all"* was that these workers were paid the prevailing wage as required by law. One Indian "body shop" got about 600 *"special visas,"* for programmers each paid only $26,500– *pay not indicative of being anything near special in skill and talent.*

"The firms lying on their forms are often those foreign suppliers. ...commonly called body shops. ...that pick the programmers, then get them their visas and assign them to the American companies," Stahl said. [568] And she told how our government wasn't tracking the number of visas, and failed to penalize companies that lied to get visa applicants approved.

Stahl explained how H-1B workers evaded paying US taxes. They lived on an allowance in the US and transferred their salary to India. Their total pay was less than $20,000 a year. [568] As a result many H-1Bs *lived in the US tax free, benefiting from technology and infrastructure built and paid for by Americans.*

H-1B fraud was traced to business lobbies that pressured our government, reported Stahl. Congress was considering a proposal by the *Clinton administration to require that Americans be hired first.* [568] (*Also see in 1998 Clinton did a flip flop and was worse than Bush.*)

60 Minutes H-1B Flip Flop–What Happened in 2003?

After exposing the H-1B visa fraud, ten years later 60 Minutes did a flip flop when it broadcasted, "Imported from India" in 2003. This show was PR for importing H-1B visa workers from India. [323]

It began with Lesley Stahl elevating India's IIT as being better than Harvard, MIT, and Princeton all combined. She called our Ivy League schools "*safety schools*" for Indians who can't get into IIT. [323]

> Only one IIT university made it to the list of Top 500 Research Institutes. IIT Kharagpur was 403 on the list. The top ranked research institutes were Harvard, Stanford, Cambridge, UC Berkeley and MIT. We had 170 universities in the list. [523] i.e. 60 Minutes was providing false information with regard to how our universities compared to India's.

Vinod Khosla, an immigrant from India, was introduced as "*one of Silicon Valley's most important venture capitalists.*" He told Stahl that immigrants from India had created hundreds of thousands of jobs. [323] Stahl should have asked *how many of these jobs were filled by hiring H-1Bs*; and, if the jobs were "created" or taken from Americans. Stahl failed to make the connection when he also *said that H-1B workers from India* "*are favored over almost anybody else.*" Khosla even said: "*If you are a WASP (White Anglo-Saxon Protestant) walking in for a job, you wouldn't have as much pre-assigned credibility as you do if you're an engineer from the Indian Institute of Technology.*" [323] This was discriminating against US citizens on the basis of race, religion, and nationality. [55] [125]

- ■ *One month after the show was aired, "Lawsuit Slams Sun's 'Bias' for Indian H-1B Workers" reported Sun Microsystems, co-founded by Khosla, laid off 2,500 Americans.* [55]

- ■ *Khosla's superiority claims were bogus—Java, Sun's leading software for the Internet was developed by James Gosling—a white guy. In 2005, Gosling was Sun's CTO for creating products for developers.* [478]

A glimmer of the truth is finally revealed when Khosla said, "*India now is benefiting significantly from the cycling of knowledge.*" [323] Cycling or Siphoning? What knowledge did we get from India?

"*IIT undergraduates leave their American counterparts in the dust,*" Stahl declared. [323] She called IIT graduates, "*India's most valuable export.*" Then she asked why India would spend $2,800 per year (totaling $11,200 for a 4 year IIT degree) and then "export" them to the US. [323]

- *The math of why India would do this is simple. If India can "export" an H-1B paid $50,000 a year who transfers 40% back home to India, then India would get $20,000 per year—almost double India's investment in the first year. After that it is all gravy for India's economy. Note: ten years later H-1B's pay had increased to about $50K per year.*

Narayan Murthy, *founder of Infosys an India outsourcing company,* told Stahl that IIT graduates' big goal is to <u>penetrate the management ranks of Corporate America. Once in position they are to "persuade" US corporations to "start operations in India.</u>" He said IIT's had succeeded in selling offshoring to US corporations such as: Texas Instruments, General Electric, and Citibank. [323]

- *Murthy is "an IT advisor to several Asian countries" BusinessWeek listed him in "The Stars of Asia"; and 1999 entrepreneur of the year. Ernst & Young named him 2003 World Entrepreneur of the Year. Fortune magazine named him "2003 Asia's Businessmen of the Year."* [601] *How did a US job outsourcer get so many US media awards?*

REBUTTALS TO "IMPORTED FROM INDIA"

Dr. Norman Matloff called "Imported From India" "*a fawning, unbalanced <u>advertisement under the guise of "news,</u>"*" and speculated the story was "*deliberately set up by expensive PR firms*" to promote India's "*Brand IIT.*" 60 Minutes responded that the show was done <u>at the request of an Indian doctor</u> not a PR firm. [324] Murthy said his son was rejected by IIT, but got into Cornell. Matloff discovered the secret behind Murthy's son's admission to Cornell–*Murthy was on the Cornell University Council.* Matloff also found that *Murthy contradicted his 60 Minutes comments–in an India magazine article. Murthy chastised IIT students because Americans repeatedly outperformed them.* [324]

Despite complaints by viewers, 60 Minutes failed to air letters of dissent as it had in the past. Matloff said <u>our media was being manipulated by "corporate and political interests.</u>" [327]

60 Minutes—2004 Offshoring PR Piece!

The following year in 2004, a *60 Minutes* story "Out of India" promoted offshoring our jobs to India! *"India is Nirvana"* for US companies, said Morley Safer. Why? India cranks out a million college graduates a year they can *hire much cheaper than American workers.* He said: *"India epitomizes the new global economy."* [308] Safer interviewed people profiting from offshoring to India.

Raman Roy, chairman of Wipro, one of India's big outsourcing companies, told Safer that US companies save 30 to 50% offshoring customer service calls to India. Roy said we should accept offshoring because *the economy is global and geography is irrelevant. But then contradictorily he said offshoring* has given India *"a terrific sense of national pride ... a huge amount of nationalistic pride."* [308] What about USA pride?

Safer did not object when workers in India told him how they were trained to deceive Americans to make them think they were talking with someone in the United States. [308]

Partha Iyengar an analyst in India told Safer: *"The reason the (US) companies are coming here is to really be more competitive and that cannot be bad for the U.S. economy."* He called it the *"__outsourcing revolution__"* and claimed India has tapped into the US *"knowledge industry."* [308]

Arjun Raina taught workers in India how to pressure Americans for debt collections. He told Safer they were polite at first and used an American accent. However, Raina said the good part was when they could forget the fake accent and get aggressive. [308] How ironic and demeaning for Americans, who lost their jobs to foreign workers, to then have foreign workers call and harass them to pay bills.

Dave Wyle told Safer that Sureprep, a company he set up in India to process US tax returns, had over 150 US accounting firms as clients. To his credit Safer said: *"But most people regard their tax returns as among the most private things they have. Is there any risk of that security being broken with tax returns flying though the ozone?"* [308]

Information Week Attacked Visa Critics

Not only did the media not cover the job losses caused by the H-1B program, it aggressively belittled H-1B critics who tried to protect American workers from the fraud.

For instance, Dr. Matloff, noted a *"rank conflict of interest"* in a 2004 InformationWeek article. The story attacked critics of H-1B and L-1 visas using a Carnegie Mellon University's Software Industry Center (SIC) "study." Matloff found that Tata Consultancy Services (TCS), an Indian outsourcing company employing H-1Bs and L-1s, is a founding partner of and *holds a seat on SIC's board.* Matloff said the study was done by a *"codirector of SIC not just a researcher."* The study was cited in the *Washington Post* praising the H-1B program. [464]

Why Did Our Media Cover-up the H-1B?

"US Companies Quietly Moving More Jobs Overseas," a 2003 Reuters article, reported that companies worried that it was not *"politically correct to talk about it."* [100] More importantly, it exposed that *major US media companies are also involved in outsourcing and offshoring including: Walt Disney Co, Time Warner, CNN, and Fox News "none of which want public disclosure."* [100]

So, executives don't want you to know about H-1Bs and offshoring. And, *our media is not going to tell you–because our media is also hiring H-1Bs and offshoring.* As a result what you are getting are global news networks promoting "globalization," when you need American news networks looking out for the interests of Americas.

What can you do? Write to your representatives and get other people to write also. Demand media reform. Corporations should not own and control the media reporting on them, nor should our media be so consolidated that it is controlled by a few people.

Chapter 5

Executive Greed

"For the love of money is the root of all kinds of evil." 1 Timothy 6:10

From the 1950's-1980 we enjoyed phenomenal economic success spearheaded by the strategies of leading American management consultants.

Then in 1980, American management consultants began to sound alarms about executives exploiting companies to take excessive compensation. For example, Peter Drucker, a renowned US management consultant and US university professor, warned that the growing pay gap between CEO pay and worker pay in large corporations could lead to exploitation and dishonesty. *CEO pay had soared to 42 times the pay of ordinary workers.* [3]

Did our government heed the warnings? No.

It allowed the average CEO pay to worker pay ratio to grow more than tenfold, reaching *458 times worker pay by the year 2000, at the peak of the dotcom boom.* [2]

But these were brilliant managers and deserved the pay right?

No. A study of executive pay from 1980 to 2000 found that the *highest paid executives were below market performance* both during the rise and the fall of our stock market. [2]

Want to Know What Happened?

As our economy declined and our debt to foreign nations grew, executive compensation skyrocketed to record levels based on financial reports. How were financial reports showing such astounding returns while in reality the companies were being mismanaged into financial crisis?

Executives artificially inflated financial statements by: claiming cost saving from displacing American workers with H-1Bs, by hyping stock using our media, by offshoring to take advantage of US tax deferments, and by other deceptive "cost savings."

Executives pursuing outsourcing were propagandized in our media as brilliant strategists re-engineering business processes. Enron was one among many companies that employed H-1Bs, engaged in offshoring, and categorized outsourcing as a *"New Economy"* strategy. Clinton praised Ken Lay in 1997 for the *"diversity"* that would keep Enron on the *"New Economy track."* [286] When Enron's house-of-cards came tumbling down, Enron's finance chief pleaded guilty to conspiracy. *He admitted Enron executives schemed together to mislead investors so they could enrich themselves.*

Enron's fall and the dotcom crash epitomized the corruption famous economist John Kenneth Galbraith predicted years earlier. Galbraith labeled corrupt executives *"financial craftsmen"* because they seized control of corporations away from the stockholders. How? By manipulating financial documents *to make it almost impossible to monitor and audit their trail of deception.* Galbraith warned that these executives and the people they hired *assumed almost absolute power over the corporation.*

While Galbraith had predicted the problem, *what surprised him in 2002 was the magnitude of the damage* [1]

He probably did not factor in the enormity of damage caused by executives transferring US jobs, technology, and money to foreign countries to inflate their compensation.

"Can You Trust Anybody Anymore?"

"Can You Trust Anybody Anymore?" was a 2002 *Businessweek.com* report. It noted that executives did not work alone to deceive investors. The very people who were supposed to be protecting you from crime compromised their integrity for a piece of the action. Executives had help from <u>*"accountants, lawyers, bankers, legislators, even regulators*</u> ..." Complex financial schemes and massive documents obscured the truth. [8] Part of the game was to secretly sell company stocks while deceptively inflating the stock prices. [11]

In his 2004 *fortune.com* article "the Great CEO Pay Heist," Geoffrey Colvin criticized how groups of people in fiduciary roles conspired together to take excessive compensation. He faulted the <u>*"perverse interaction of CEOs, boards, consultants, even the feds.*</u>" [9]

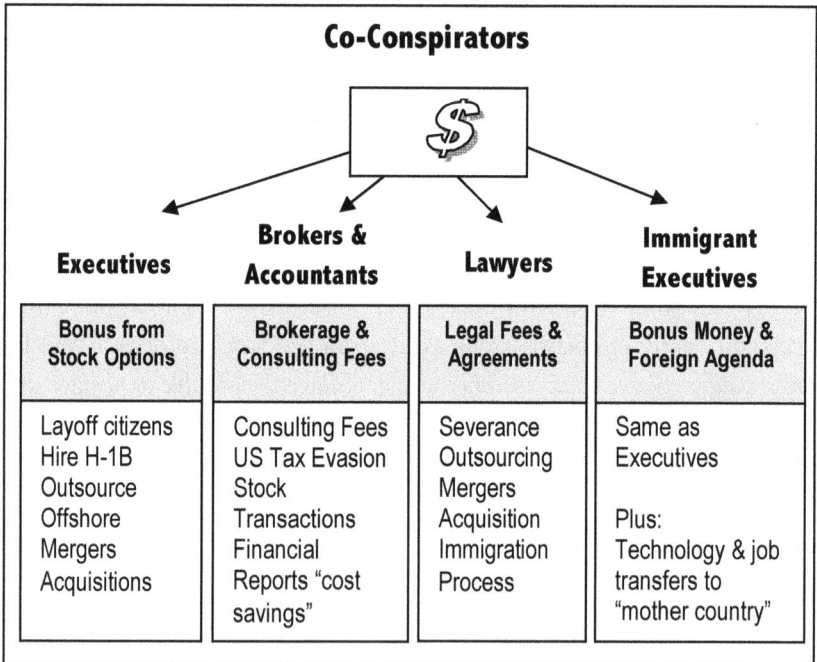

Co-Conspirators

Executives	Brokers & Accountants	Lawyers	Immigrant Executives
Bonus from Stock Options	Brokerage & Consulting Fees	Legal Fees & Agreements	Bonus Money & Foreign Agenda
Layoff citizens Hire H-1B Outsource Offshore Mergers Acquisitions	Consulting Fees US Tax Evasion Stock Transactions Financial Reports "cost savings"	Severance Outsourcing Mergers Acquisition Immigration Process	Same as Executives Plus: Technology & job transfers to "mother country"

You Get Laid Off. They Get a Bonus!

Several studies found CEO pay increases correlated with American layoffs.

- *"CEO Ponzi Scheme–Up, Up and Away: CEO Compensation" in 2000 found a 50% correlation of mass layoffs, and within 3 years CEO being listed in BusinessWeek's top 10 highest paid executives. [2]*

- *"New CEO/Worker Pay Gap Study" in 2001 reported that CEO's who laid off a thousand or more Americans were paid on average almost 80% more. [5]*

- *"For CEOs, Offshoring Pays" in 2004 cited a study that found CEOs offshoring US jobs increased their compensation by an average of 46%. It reported the CEO of Intuit got a 425% pay increase to $22.3 million while offshoring business process outsourcing (BPO) jobs to India. [4]*

- *"Executive Excess 2004—Campaign Contributions, Outsourcing, Unexpensed Stock Options and Rising CEO Pay," correlated CEO pay to layoffs for: General Electric, United Technologies, Bank of America, American Express, Oracle, and many more. Most of the jobs went to India. [6] India's highest paid was Wipro CEO who got $1 million. [271]*

- *"Executive Excess 2007" named executives receiving excessive compensation including private equity hedge funds managers. The report provided a list of proposals.*

Corporate Tax Welfare

Corporate tax welfare takes the form of <u>tax breaks for executive stock options, offshore corporate tax shelters, and other tax breaks</u>. Citizens for Tax Justice found that from 1996-2000, ten major US corporations received $50 billion in tax breaks. The report criticized the "stimulus bill" claiming that <u>Americans would be subsidizing corporations by more than $17 billion a year</u>. [156]

- *The report calculated corporate tax welfare for the following companies: Microsoft $12 billion, General Electric almost $12 billion, Ford $9.1 billion, WorldCom $5.3 billion, IBM $4.7 billion, General Motors $3.6 billion, and Enron $1 billion. [156]*

"Campaign Contributions" Pay Big Rewards

IPS found 25 companies where *"chief executive compensation actually ran higher than the company's entire federal corporate income tax bill,"* according to "Executive Excess 2011: The Massive CEO Rewards for Tax Dodging." [971]

During our recession executive pay levels increased. How did they do that?

The report noted that while executives claimed they were breaking no laws, *"massive corporate outlays for lobbying and campaign contributions"* were ***shaping the law.*** [971]

Moreover, the study exposed that: *"offshore tax gaming has spawned a massive global tax avoidance industry, with teams of lawyers and accountants who add nothing... **This "shadow" banking industry played a key role in the 2008 financial crisis.**"* For example, Citigroup and Bank of America, *"The two biggest bank recipients of US taxpayer bailouts"* –*"Citigroup operates 427 subsidiaries in tax havens, and Bank of America 115."* [971]

So US banks offshoring triggered our financial crisis, and then we Americans were taxed to bail them out.

Influence buying was not new. An earlier study estimated that 350 CEO's between 1997-2004 got $9.7 billion in stock options—*$3.9 billion of this money came from tax deductions linked to stock options.* [6]

"Government Contractors Wield Influence through Revolving Door, Campaign Contributions," a *Project on Government Oversight* report, exposed that from 1997 to 2004 the top 20 federal contractors spent $436 million on lobbying and political campaigns. *These contractors averaged receiving approximately $100 in contract awards for every 8 cents they "contributed."* Where else in the world could a company get that kind of sales volume on its marketing expenditures. This is not done directly–the contributions were not tied to specific contract awards. [440]

Where Was Congress?

Congress is supposed to protect you from corruption.

While Americans were losing their jobs and their homes, members of Congress were quite comfortable according *USAToday* article, "Lawmakers Prosper Despite Economic Slump." [737] They were living large despite the fact that corporate welfare laws, visa laws and other laws they passed are mainly responsible for our economic crisis. Do they not realize their wealth will not survive the collapse of our economy?

Seeking Justice

Don't be fooled by the 99% rhetoric that lumps all executives together. We have many talented executives who earn their income and create jobs for Americans. However, executives who have mismanaged our corporations need to be replaced by managers who will look out for the best interests of Americans. Politicians who sponsored harmful legislation need to be replaced.

This chapter was to help you see how corruption in some business and political leaders caused our job losses. Talk with your family and friends about how to clean up the corruption and create more jobs.

Chapter 6

US Economic & Tax Losses

They call losses profits.

This chapter holds the key to showing politicians and executives why it is important for them to make sure you have a good paying job. It gives you a tool to debunk the "cost savings" claimed for displacing you with a visa worker, or an offshore worker.

Remind them that you and other Americans like you are the American consumers they depend on to spend money to stimulate our economy. [72]

Remind our politicians concerned about Social Security being solvent, that when you have a job you pay into Social Security. And, if you don't have a job you don't pay into Social Security.

Also, to protect your Social Security investment you should know that many H-1Bs evade paying US taxes while working six years in the United States and then are awarded green cards entitling them to Social Security benefits when they retire. Ask your representatives what they have done to make sure H-1Bs pay their fair share into Social Security? [154]

There are attempts by foreign countries to exempt visa workers from paying US taxes. If H-1Bs are exempted from paying Social Security taxes this would give H-1Bs an insurmountable competitive cost advantage over you.

India Dominates the H-1B Visas

So who's taking our jobs? India dominates the H-1B program taking almost half the visas, followed by China with around ten percent of the visas. *Aside from India and China, H-1B visa workers came from other countries including: the UK, Canada, Philippines, Korea, Taiwan, Japan, Pakistan, Russia, and many more—each of these countries received 4% or less of the H-1Bs granted.* [41] [59]

India used a McKinsey & Company "study" released in 2003 by NASSCOM to claim that the H-1B program and outsourcing would continue, *because H-1Bs from India paid $500 million a year into US Social Security, and spent $1.8 billion a year benefiting the US economy.* On the other hand, India acknowledged that vast numbers of H-1Bs obtained green cards which will let them collect Social Security benefits when they retire. [123]

The study failed to mention that one month earlier India pressured our government to refund Social Security taxes to H-1Bs forced to return to India. Many lost jobs because of the US economic slowdown. [86] Ironically, much of our slowdown was caused by–offshoring our professional jobs to India. [123]

The McKinsey study also failed to mention that non-immigrant visa workers from India *transferred $10 billion a year in remittances from the US to India.* [28] *If half of these money transfers ($5 billion) were sent by H-1Bs to India, and H-1Bs were spending only $1.8 billion in the US, then H-1Bs were transferring about 74% of their US pay to India.*

This seems impossible until you learn that often outsourcing companies provide H-1Bs with free apartments and food, and paid them cash or a check with no US taxes withheld. Some H-1Bs have their paychecks automatically deposited in a bank in India while they live on a spending allowance and pay no US taxes. [154]

India Dominates High Tech Offshore Outsourcing

Interestingly, India calls sending H-1Bs to the US "exports." A 2001 *forbes.com* article, "Can India Retain Its Reign as Outsourcing King?" reported that India had $6 Billion in software exports. China was second with $1 billion in software exports. Pakistan was also getting $120 million in software exports. [91]

"Offshore Upstarts" a 2002 *eWeek report*, claimed <u>India was the number one source for offshoring with 85% of the software outsourcing market</u>.

[774] "Will India Price Itself Out of the Offshore Market," a 2004 report exposed that the wages for programmers in India were rapidly growing. India still had 80% of the offshore market. [301]

Months prior to our 2004 election, a *timesofindia.indiatimes.com* article, "American IT Pros Sue, Bangalore Shivers," reported that thirty five laid-off American IT professionals filed a class-action lawsuit against the US government. Programmers who lost their jobs to India wanted the same unemployment benefits that manufacturing workers got when they lost jobs to China. They wanted the "Trade Adjustment Act" to pay them *up to 2 years of unemployment, plus assistance with job training, job searches, and health insurance.* India "shivered" because the globalization deception was being exposed. [71]

Offshoring Depressed Wages & Tax Revenues

Foreign workers depressed American wages which in turn reduced taxes collected by our government. Tax revenues fell as worker pay fell from $6.35 trillion in 2000, to about $6 trillion in 2002, a 5.1% drop. The *income of Americans adjusted for inflation dropped 9.2% from 2000 to 2002. <u>Hardest hit were our high tech professional jobs.</u>* [142]

In 2005, another study also found that our standard of living was being lowered. New jobs being added were paying 21% lower wages and were providing less health insurance or none at all. <u>*The hardest hit professions were US software jobs.*</u> [141]

Economic Reality Check

If the claims of foreign worker cost savings benefits were real, then areas with high concentrations of foreign visa workers would have the greatest prosperity in America.

California is the litmus test state because it has the most foreign IT workers. California's budget deficit hit $35 billion in 2003. [197] California continued to run multi-billion dollar deficits. By 2011, despite deep cuts in spending, California was projected to run a $21 billion deficit in 2012. [985] *California's budget shortfall, still the worst in our nation, shows the real economic impact.*

Prior to the influx of foreign workers, Silicon Valley was one of the most prosperous areas in the US. California was well positioned to maintain its prosperity and our nation's high tech leadership. Instead, California has been decimated by layoffs of US citizens displaced by foreign workers.

This pattern of economic decline followed in other states as H-1B workers displaced American workers. For example, North Carolina went from a prosperous state to running billion dollar budget deficits.

Bottom line, Americans fund the US Government by paying a percent of their income in taxes. Diminishing Americans' income weakens our Government because it has less money for defense, less money for research, less money for Social Security, less money for education, and less money for other programs.

A 2004, *cbsnews.com* report, "Outsourcing Backlash Brewing," said: "*Despite the daunting economic logic, outsourcing opponents say they hope to educate the public about the true cost of globalization.*" [72] The following Economic Circulation Model™ was created to take on the "*daunting economic logic,*" and expose the "*true cost of globalization.*" This model holds the key to our jobs recovery.

Economic Circulation Model=Key to Recovery

If you are given bad advice and go down a perilous one lane road and hit a dead end, the only way out is to carefully reverse course. Our leaders followed deceptive advice and drove us down the *'transfer jobs to "cheaper" foreign workers'* dead end road. It is time to reverse.

Using the Economic Circulation Model, let's compute our tax and business losses caused by displacing one American IT worker that we will call Sam, with a foreign visa worker from India. In this analysis, Sam is paid $80,000 per year compared with an H-1B or L-1 visa worker paid $50,000 per year.

First let's compute the economic and tax impact of Sam's job.

Sam's Direct Economic Impact in the United States	
Salary	$80,000
State Taxes	$5,600
Federal Taxes 28%	$22,400
After-Tax Income Spent (Circulated in the US)	$52,000

If Sam pays $22,400 in federal taxes, plus $5,600 for state taxes he pays a total of $28,000 in US taxes (While not all states collect income taxes; all do find ways to collect money to fund schools, roads, and other infrastructure.)

After Sam pays his taxes, *he has $52,000 left to spend.*

Cycle 1 is where Sam buys goods and services from US businesses such as his mortgage lender, his grocer, his doctor, his barber, and other businesses. This puts his money in circulation.

Cycle 2 is when Americans who received money from selling to Sam, pay taxes on the money, and then spend the remainder buying goods and services from US businesses.

The cycles continue as long as there is after-tax money to spend.

The following chart shows income put into circulation by Sam. *Each time the money changes hands in the United States, our government collects more taxes, and our businesses make more money.*

Economic Circulation Model™ of Sam's Job
Money Circulated Generating US Taxes & US Business Income

	Cycle 1	Cycle 2	Cycle 3	Cycle 4	Cycle 5	Totals
Income Circulated	$52,000	$33,800	$21,970	$14,281	$9,282	$131,333
State Tax	$3,640	$2,366	$1,538	$1,000	$650	$9,193
Fed Tax	$14,56	$9,464	$6,152	$3,999	$2,599	$36,773
After-Tax Income to Recycle	$33,800	$21,970	$14,281	$9,282	$6,034	

(Note when the after-tax income fell to $6,034 calculations were stopped to fit the chart on the page.)

So Sam's after tax money he spent in the USA circulated and generated approximately $46,000 in taxes ($9,193 State Tax + $36,773 Federal Tax). If you add the $46,000 to the $28,000 Sam paid, the total taxes collected by our government is $74,000.

The amazing fact is that when the money circulates in our economy it is taxed over and over again, and the US government collects taxes almost as much as Sam's total pay.

The impact from Sam spending his $52,000 buying in the USA is even greater. The money circulates *pumping $131,000 into the US economy as income for American businesses.*

So the overall economic and tax benefit of Sam's $80,000 salary is $74,000 in taxes plus $131,000 for a total impact of *$205,000.*

Think of it like this. If you are an adult, you have about 10 pints of blood, yet your heart pumps about 2,000 gallons a day. The same blood circulates over and over again replenishing your body. And, while it can be a good thing to donate blood to help other people, it is a bad thing to take too much out of circulation, you will collapse.

WHAT HAPPENS WHEN SAM LOSES HIS JOB TO AN H-1B?

An H-1B paid $50,000 a year is supposed to pay 40% in US taxes or $20,000. [30] [46] However, many H-1Bs pay little or no US taxes. [30] [46] [153] For example, some H-1Bs are paid minimum wage salaries while they are *paid separately for US living expenses which are not taxable.* [28]

A tax treaty exempts H-1B Chinese teachers or research assistants in US universities from taxes. [58] Moreover, some visa workers, such as L-1 visa workers are regarded as employees of a foreign owned company, so *even though they take jobs in the United States they do not have to pay US income taxes.* [28] [143]

As a result, "high paid" Americans like you and like Sam who pay 28%+ in taxes frequently bring home less pay than foreign workers who evade paying taxes. Americans need higher base salaries than foreign workers, because we don't get the tax breaks exploited by foreign visa workers. We can't deduct our living expenses.

As noted earlier, money transfers that visa workers send back to India *appear to average about 74% of their salary.* For the sake of simplicity, we will assume that if a visa worker from India pays 40% in US taxes they only transfer 40% of their salary to India; and that if they pay no US taxes they transfer 80% back to India i.e. we assume the money they did not pay in US taxes is transferred to India. (The average of 80% and 40% = 60% which is 14% below 74%.)

If the H-1B transfers $20,000 back home to India and pays $20,000 in US taxes, that leaves only $10,000 to

	H-1 B Visa Worker	H-1B or L-1 Visa No Taxes Paid
Salary	$50,000	$50,000
US Taxes Paid 40%	$20,000	$0
Transfer to India	$20,000	$40,000
Money to be Circulated in the US	$10,000	$10,000

spend in the United States. Or, if the visa worker paid no US taxes and transferred 80% to India, that also leaves only $10,000 to spend.

Feeding $10,000 into the Economic Circulation Model generates only about $16,500 in the US business earnings and about $6,000 in US tax revenue. If the H-1B visa worker paid US taxes, add the $20,000 they paid plus $6,000 and the total is only $26,000. If they paid no taxes, then the US tax revenues are only $6,000.

Economic Circulation Model of Foreign H-1B or L1 Visa Worker

	Cycle 1	Cycle 2	Cycle 3	Cycle 4	Cycle 5	Totals
Income Circulated	$10,000	$6,500				$16,500
State Tax	$700	$455				$1,155
Fed Tax	$2,800	$1,820				$4,620
After-Tax Income to Recycle	$6,500	$4,225				

Now we can calculate the impact to the US government, and US businesses from displacing Sam with an H-1B.

US Tax & Economic Losses

	Sam's Tax & Economic Contributions	H-1B's Tax & Economic Contributions	Losses from Displacing Sam with an H-1B
Taxes Paid Directly	$28,000	$20,000*	
Taxes Generated by Money Circulated in US	$46,000	$6,000	
Total US Taxes	$74, 000	$26,000	$48,000
US Business Income from Circulated Income	$131,000	$16,500	$114,500
Total Tax & Economic Impact	$205,000	$42,500	$162,500

*If an L-1 Visa worker or an H-1 that evaded US taxes delete this amount, increasing the yearly loss to **$182,500**.

Our politicians should note that while Sam would have generated $74,000 in taxes, a visa worker would have generated only $26,000 for a net tax loss of $48,000 per year; or worse. If the H-1B paid no US taxes $68,000.

US business owners should note the economic damage caused by displacing Sam with a visa worker. Sam's $131,000 minus the H-1Bs $16,500 and the US business economic loss is $114,500 per year.

Overall our tax and economic loss is $162,500 per year from displacing Sam with an H-1B; or, if the visa worker paid no taxes then the loss to the United States is $182,500 per year.

The amazing fact is that the indirect loss from transferring money out of circulation in the United States is much greater than the direct loss. And this economic loss of $162,500–$182,500 is the impact from replacing just one American IT worker with a foreign visa worker. So hiring "cheaper" visa workers may pad the pockets of a few executives, but it greatly harms our government and overall economy.

So how many Americans lost their jobs to foreign visa workers? By 2001, the number of H-1Bs in the US was estimated between 2-4 million. So if we lost 3 million jobs at an estimated cost of $162,500 each, the total economic and tax loss ($162,500 * 3 million) is $487.5 billion per year. Next, we need to add an estimate for L-1 and other visa workers and illegal aliens. If all these combined total another 3 million jobs, then an additional $487.5 billion is lost per year. Bringing our combined US *economic and tax losses to almost $1 trillion per year.*

Our *real losses are even greater*, because the model does not include: layoff costs such as unemployment payments, uninsured US citizens, retraining costs, welfare costs, and more. Nor does the model include defaults on mortgage payments, car payments; credit card payments ... [154] And, the worst loss of all is the impact on American children and broken families. The visa damage is enormous and unsustainable. It must be carefully and quickly reversed to restore our economy.

Calculating US Economic Losses from Offshoring

What about the cost saving from replacing Americans with offshore foreign workers? The offshore foreign worker would pay no US taxes, and would spend no money in the US.

All the US businesses that sold products and services to Sam such as: the restaurants where he eats, the grocery stores where he shops would get nothing.

Economic Damage From Offshoring Sam's Job
No Taxes Collected and No Money Circulated

	Cycle 1	Cycle 2	Cycle 3	Cycle 4	Cycle 5	Totals
Income Circulated	$0	$0				$0
State Tax	$0					$0
Federal Tax	$0					$0
After Tax Income to Recycle	$0					

So the overall loss to the US from Sam losing a job to an offshore worker is the full <u>$205,000 per year for each job loss.</u>

This economic model shows the criticality of keeping Americans like you employed. The "cost savings" from replacing an American with a "cheaper" offshore worker is a deceptive illusion.

Think of it this way. When Sam's IT job is lost, approximately three to four support jobs are also lost. On a larger scale this phenomenon can be observed when a factory in a small town closes. It is not just the factory workers who lose jobs. The whole town suffers; from grocery stores, to clothing stores, to home builders, and other businesses.

The following graphic provides a visual of the awful damage caused by each transfer of an Americans' job to a foreign worker. Offshoring literally flat lines our government and economy.

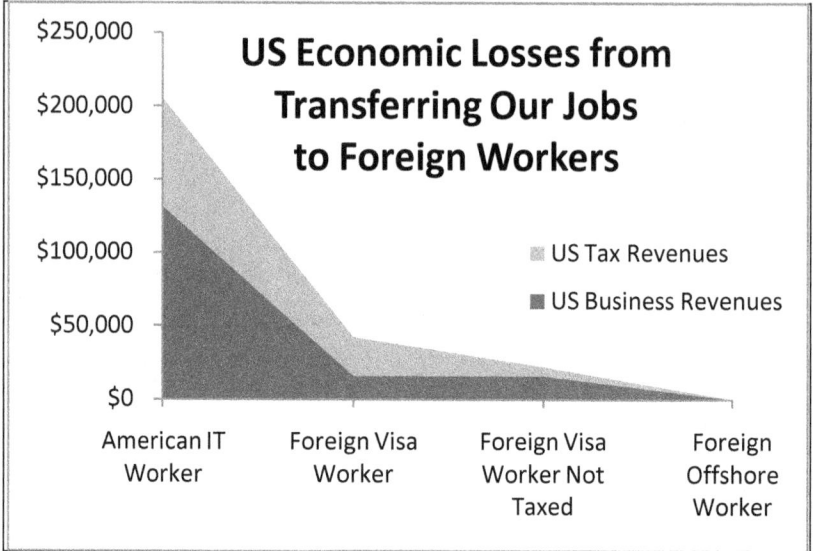

The next question is how many American jobs have been offshored and how big are the projections for offshoring? Surprisingly our government has not been tracking the number of these job losses.

Offshoring accelerated dramatically after the dotcom crash. If around 5 million jobs were offshored, then $205,000 * 5 million would be a yearly economic and tax loss of about $1,025 billion.

Multiple sources projected that 14 million US white collar jobs were at risk of being offshored. If 14 million US jobs are offshored, then $205,000 * 14 million would result in future ___US economic and tax losses of almost $3 Trillion per year!___ This is a big bite out of the annual *$15 trillion GDP for the entire US.* Note that these are the high paying jobs. The financial impact of one $80,000 per year job is equivalent to losing four jobs that pay $20,000 per year.

It is Time to Stop and Reverse

The important point is that this economic model focuses on the impact for each individual job taken.

This Economic Circulation Model™ is a tool for you to use to disprove the cost savings claims used to justify displacing you with a foreign worker. These computations were focused on our high tech job losses. The same economic model can be used to estimate the costs of other American job losses. For example, manufacturing jobs have been transferred at disturbing rates as have business processes (BPO) jobs such as customer support, insurance claims processing, and more.

The good news is that this economic model also works in reverse. If we require companies to post pending green card applications, and jobs filled by H-1Bs these jobs can be reclaimed. Millions of Americans who are unemployed and underemployed could fill the jobs.

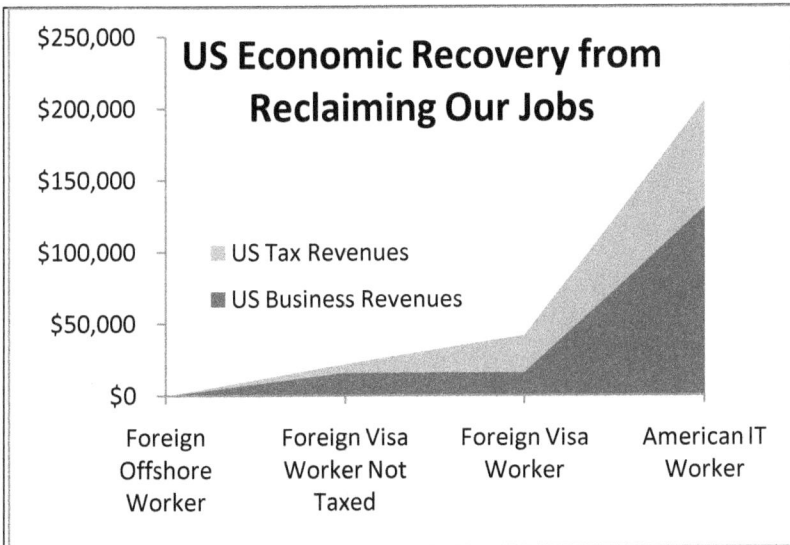

We can rebound more quickly that many people think.

Chapter 7

Americans Taxed To Educate

Competition

Americans were taxed to fund educating foreign students who took their jobs.

Where did all these foreign visa workers competing with you for jobs come from? They were educated in our universities at our expense. According to a September 2004, "War Outsourcing and Debt Delusion Rules," by Paul Craig Roberts, *US universities had educated enough people from India and China to take every high tech job American corporations needed.* [255]

Foreign student graduates took entry level high tech job opportunities away from young Americans. When executives channeled jobs to foreign workers, they denied job opportunities to young Americans graduating with college degrees in science and engineering. [47] [88] Without entry level high tech job experience young Americans will not develop the skills necessary to design the technology of the future. [255]

Corporate executives hired foreign graduates and claimed it was justified, because America invested in their education. They warned that if these foreign students returned to their country they would compete against America. [255] It's time we invest in our own kids.

Taxed to Educate Our Competition

Do you want to know how we have been taxed to fund college for millions of foreign students? [230] US colleges are subsidized by our taxes. Tuition and other *bills paid by students* do not usually cover the full costs. For example, in 2002, it was estimated that we subsidized students attending public universities on average $9,200 per student. So, *500,000 foreign students in our universities cost almost $5 billion a year, even if they pay full tuition, room and board and other expenses.* [230]

But that's not all. As recently as 2004, the National Center for Education Statistics reported that the majority of foreign graduate got financial assistance including grants that they do not have to repay. [252] [143] A professor at the University of California wrote that, *a foreign graduate student in a 4-6 year PhD program costs about $120,000 to $220,000 in grant money.* [549] If 300,000 foreign students get these grants, that's *$36 to $66 billion dollars!*

While we are taxed to fund foreign students, many foreign students are exempt from paying US taxes. For example one study reported that, *"Students from India are given an exemption from paying taxes."* [143] How is that fair to young Americans and their parents?

We are even taxed to recruit foreign students. The *US State Dept. set up over 450 centers around the globe to recruit foreign students,* and it funds EducationUSA which provides information on how to get visas, and *how to apply for financial aid.* [477] Our National Science Foundation encourages US universities to recruit foreign students. [186]

"U.S. Schools, Foreign Enrollments Soar," a 2008 *usatoday.com* article challenged claims that foreign students provide a financial benefit. It reported that the costs of educating foreign students are understated. And, that *US universities provide financial aid to 90.7% of foreign graduate students and only 64% of American graduate students.* Ultimately it warned foreign students depress wages and discourage Americans from pursuing graduate studies in key fields. [726]

Out of Control Student Visa Increases

While many foreign students are wonderful people, and it can be great to learn about their cultures; _when we host too many they take educational opportunities from our own children. And, the costs to educate them unfairly burdens middle class Americans._

For years we have hosted more foreign students than any other country in the world. [967]

- From 1955 to 2004 foreign student enrollment in our colleges climbed 1,572%! Foreign students in this volume pose a major economic drain and national security risk to our country. [252]

- Another dramatic jump in foreign student enrollment occurred in 2005, dominated by Asians who took 58% of the student visas. [531]

- In 2008, a record 623,805 foreign students were enrolled in US colleges.

- From 2009-2010, the number of foreign students hit another record reaching 690,923. China increased enrollment by 30% sending 128,000 students. India was in second place sending 105,000.

Why? Our State Department "_made it a priority to reach out to talented international students, particularly students from disadvantaged backgrounds. A global education prepares them to become leaders in their own countries and societies._ " [967] The reality is that few return to their own countries.

The number of student visas soared to 723,277 in 2011! Chinese enrollments jumped to 158,000. India's student enrollments in our universities hit 104,000. Many foreign students brought along family members. [980] The 23% jump in Chinese enrollments "_fueled anxiety among American students and their parents about increased competition._" Charles Bennett, Minister-Counselor Affairs at the US embassy claimed "_Foreign students spend about $21 billion a year in the U.S. in tuition and living expenses for them and their families._" [983] The real irony is most, if not all, the money from China and India came from outsourced US jobs.

To put these numbers in perspective, you need to know that in 1965 politicians promised Americans that the total number of immigrants admitted per year would remain at 200,000. *Foreign students alone were more than triple that amount!* What is more, student visas do not include foreign students in our country illegally, nor students using visitor visas and other visas. [252]

How can our politicians justify taxing us to fund educating foreign students taking our jobs. Given our trade deficits with China and other countries makes this even more appalling.

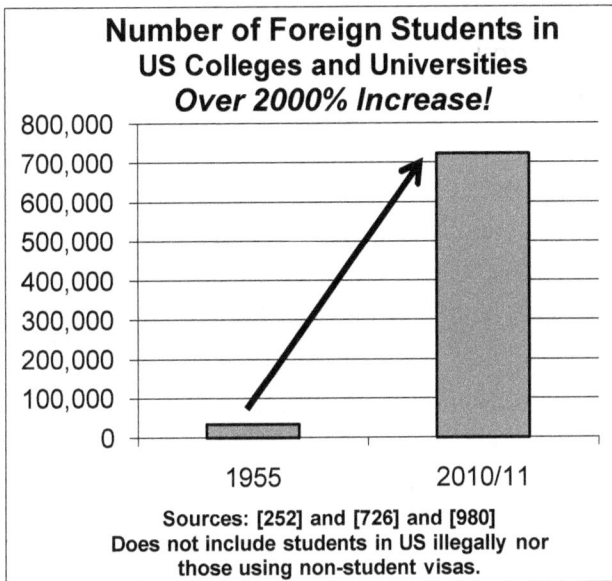

Number of Foreign Students in US Colleges and Universities
Over 2000% Increase!

Sources: [252] and [726] and [980]
Does not include students in US illegally nor those using non-student visas.

Are foreign students good for America? Not according to an evaluation by George Borjas who in 2002 wrote two articles, "Rethinking Foreign Students—A Question of National Interest" [230] and "An Evaluation of the Foreign Student Program." He found that the foreign student visa program was *"riddled with corruption"* and *"ineptly run."* [254] Proponents of student visas claim that it benefits our country by creating alliances with foreign countries. Yet there does not appear to be much evidence to support this claim.

Americans' College Costs Soared

The growing number of foreign students caused our college costs to rise. Compounding the problem, when foreign students graduated they took Americans' jobs and depressed wages. This decreased the taxes collected by our state governments, and in turn forced states to cut back on the money they gave to state universities. To offset the decline in state funding, college costs increased faster than inflation. [264] [263]

From *1985 to 2000, our college costs grew at almost 3 times the rate of the median family income*. A 2004 analysis of college costs, "U.S. Flunks Higher Education Affordability" compared average family income with net college costs. [262] Our Department of Education reported that *170,000 qualified students could not even afford the cost of a community college*. [264]

Squeezed by rising college costs parents resorted to home equity loans. This precarious financial position of putting the family home up as collateral for a college loan created substantial stress. It is hard for students to focus on studies when worrying about finances and working one or more jobs.

Even with help from their families, and working summer jobs the average American college student had to take out loans and work 23 hours a week to pay for college. In 2004, on average they graduated owing $17,000 in student loans. [264]

Student loan debt got much worse. *From 1998 to 2009 the amount of federal student loans doubled to $85 billion, and private loans tripled.* About *two thirds* graduated with *big college loans* to repay. They could not find jobs because of visa workers and offshoring. Ironically people who ran up credit card debt or even gambling debt could get bankruptcy relief— but not young Americans who invested in getting an education. [743]

In 2010 student loan debt climbed to $800 billion exceeding US credit card debt.

In 2011 *student loan debt was estimated to be a trillion dollars.* [915]

Who's a Minority?

Our universities set affirmative action goals to help *descendants of native tribes and of slaves*, who were demographically underrepresented. For example, *a group that comprises 10% of US citizens would be underrepresented if they had less than 10% of the seats in our colleges.* Our universities wrongly used *foreign students* to claim affirmative action goals: *"these foreign graduate students are particularly attractive to universities when they can use them to meet affirmative action goals."* [252] Consider the following statistics to understand the absurdity of counting students from China and India as minorities.

In 2008, it was estimated that *China produced 600,000 engineers, India 350,000 and the United States only 70,000.* [687]

In 2005, it was estimated that *China produced 50,000 computer scientists, India 68,000, and the United States 30,000.* [766] [161] [484]

Asians account from less than 3% of Americans, yet the University of California, Berkeley undergraduate program was 40% Asian in 2007. [627]

Some analysts say China and India inflate their numbers by counting people with certificates. However, even if their estimates are inflated, it appears they are producing more than the US.

So *why are critical educational opportunities in our universities going to foreign students?* [264]

Number of Engineering Graduates Produced Per Year

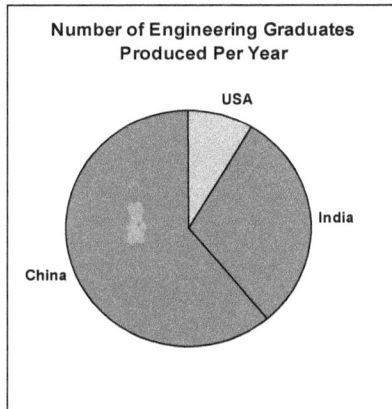

Number of Computer Science Graduates Produced Per Year

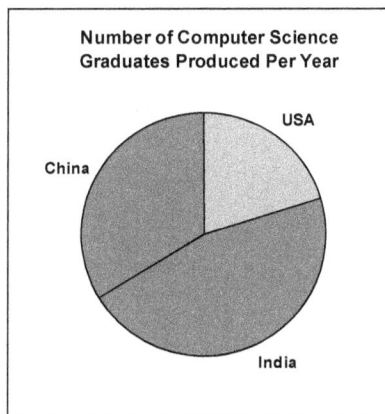

Lesser Qualified Foreign Students Favored

Claims that foreign students are superior to Americans is a deception. In reality lesser qualified foreign students take education slots that should go to highly qualified Americans. This is harming our nation's ability to compete globally.

"*Foreign students have a much easier path to being admitted to US universities and even more amazingly they get loads of aid and scholarships to attend college for free something unavailable to US citizens like you and me*" *Wayne Allyn Root said: " It's a completely different path. A path so easy that even a kid with ... no money and lousy grades can get admitted to the best colleges. Ivy League Columbia is a possibility—for a foreign student. And, **it's all paid by the taxpayers** How do you like that?"* [1020]

Root explained, "*The door magically opened for a foreign student.*" Why? Our colleges recruit "*foreigners to create diversity.*" He observed that, "*some US student, a valedictorian of his or her school who never got to go to Columbia or Harvard Law*" when a foreign student "*took their place.*" [1020]

We Paid Record Levels of Student Aid

The dual negative impact of depressing wages while at the same time increasing the number of "minorities" meant that *even though we paid a record $105 billion in student aid in 2002, the number of students applying for aid dramatically increased resulting in a decrease in the amount of aid received per student.* For example, $11.7 billion in 2002 for Pell grants was divided among 4.8 million students. [264]

Proposed Education Cost Relief for Americans

While many foreign students got a free ride on our tax dollars, college costs for American youth have soared to levels beyond reason. Americans should not have to use home equity loans or their retirement savings to pay for college. The money that has been going to foreign students needs to be redistributed to cut college costs for US citizens.

The Good News

We are being warned that we are at risk of losing our technology leadership because we are producing fewer engineering graduates than China and India. [504] While numbers sound daunting, You should not lose heart. *Most of our greatest inventors never had PhDs.* [491] Moreover, creating a glut of engineers and scientists does not encourage inventiveness, but rather hinders it as engineers and scientists vie for a limited number of jobs and worry about job security.

Over and over again Americans have proven that they have fantastic invention skills. What we need to do is to get US citizens back in our R&D labs, reward inventors with recognition and job security, take appropriate measures to protect the intellectual property they invent, and the US will do wonders again.

Chapter 8

Foreign Student Visa Fraud

Cheating degrades education.

To qualify for a student visa a foreigner must be accepted by an INS-approved school. *The INS approved 73,000 schools! In addition to universities it approved beauty schools, English language schools, acupuncture schools, etcetera.* There was not enough oversight to ensure against visa fraud. [230] The INS did not control nor track the numbers. [252]

Students were granted *temporary non-immigrant student visas (NIVs)*.

- ■ *F1 student visa holders are required by law to exit the U.S. within 60 days of completing academic studies.*

- ■ *The M1, granted for trade and vocational schools, is valid for one year.*

- ■ *The J1 for academic training "not available in their home country" is used by students, professors, teachers, physicians, and more.* [611] [612] [613]

"*The most common reason for a student or exchange visitor application to be denied is that the person applying for the visa has not proven to the Visa Officer that they will return to their country when they complete their studies in the USA.*" [1021] It is illegal to misuse student visas to immigrate. [41] Applicants were required to sign a legal agreement that they would not try to stay. If they stayed after their visa expired they became illegal aliens. The failure of our government to enforce immigration laws emboldened foreign students. The National Association of Foreign Student Advisors (NAFSA) lobby was formed to pressure our Congress to grant them US citizenship. [221]

Student Visa Application Fraud

"So prized are U.S. student visas that the deceptions used to acquire them can be elaborate ... Because visa officers <u>conduct as many as 200 interviews per day</u>, they've no time to verify documents or confirm stories" www.americanvisas.com reported. It estimated 99% of students from China tried to stay illegally. It was so bad that one former US official said: "<u>An honest evaluation would virtually end visa issuance.</u>" [246] Chinese "consulting" firms charged $10,000 to supply false reference letters, <u>fake documents showing economic support,</u> and even an actor for the interview at the US consular office. And, the Foreign Studies Service Bureau in India guaranteed a visa for about $800. [230]

A US consular official could not approve a visa application if there was any reason to suspect the student would attempt to stay in the United States. [252] However, "<u>many foreigners want to study in the U.S. precisely because a student visa buys them a ticket into the country.</u>" [230] When our government granted amnesty to 3 million illegal aliens in 1986, almost 10% were visa violators.

Foreign students frequently cheated on admission exams. One standardized exam had to stagger test times and change questions each time the test was administered because students taking the tests in California were photographing the test and posting it on the web to help students in Hong Kong cheat. [634] Moreover, Asian universities posted the answers to the English language test relied upon by American universities as the basis for foreign student admissions. [634] No wonder we have so many foreign students.

In 2010 US consular officials caught a visa applicant in India whose TOEFL scores certified high level English skills, yet she could not answer basic questions in English. She admitted to buying fraudulent documents. Business centers in India were selling "forged academic degrees." Investigators said, "the US government believes that any funds collected ... for fraudulent documents may represent **_proceeds of a crime which may be sizable_**..." [754] Many students from India violate their visas and stay illegally in our country, yet India arrests foreign students who overstay according to an article, "Hyderabad Police Arrest 25 Foreign Students for Overstaying." [716]

Tragic Rise in Cheating

If someone cheated to get admitted to college, they can be expected to cheat to get a degree. *"Large-scale cheating ... has hit US Campuses in recent years."* [628] An analysis of cheating found that in 1963 about 26% of students cheated, in 1993 the percentage more than doubled reaching 56%, and by 2007 over 70% of students cheated. [634]

The flood of foreign students into our universities, and our job markets increased the pressure to cheat. One theory is that overcrowding of our labor pool *"is the real culprit"* driving the increased cheating. Another theory is that a cultural shift may be the cause. A 2006, *Newsweek International* article, "Education: Why Everyone Cheats Now," reported that cheating on university entrance exams was common in India and China. Pre-medical exams to get into India's universities sold for $15,000. Gangs supplied "look-alikes" to take *Chinese university entrance exams* for a fee. [634]

According to national surveys *"cheating is widespread among graduate students."* [635] Imagine a student with a thick college textbook and 50 pages of notes with no idea of what questions will be on the exam, competing against someone who has an illegal copy of the exam and got help finding the answers. Unchecked cheating allows cheaters to rise to the top. *The smartest student may well be the one with the lowest score who did not cheat.*

A 2007 article, "Duke Business School Hit by Cheating Scandal," reported that a professor noticed some students' answers on a take home exam were suspiciously similar. *This triggered an investigation that caught thirty-four MBA graduate students in a network of cheating.* Students stole copies of test answers, then distributed the answers and collaborated with other students to cheat on the test. The *MBA program involved had 40% foreign students* and costs about $60,000 yr. [628]

Ohio University discovered *over 20 mechanical engineering graduate students cheated on their master's thesis.* Students were dismissed and a master's degree was revoked. [635]

Destructive Cultural Shift

Our nation is going through a catastrophic shift in culture that is shaking the very foundation of trust essential to the successful functioning of our schools, government, and stock market. The moral fabric of our society is being torn apart.

Of course, there have always been students who cheat. However, when cheating becomes the norm, not the exception, education is degraded. When many students cheat, it puts pressure on other students to cheat to remain competitive. A lot of students now believe you have to cheat to be successful. [634] Because of ethnic network collaboration, some foreign students who cheat have a big advantage over American students who cheat.

Apparently cheaters are more likely to be admitted to our universities, be promoted to management, and get rich investing in our stock market. Yet, no one wants a surgeon that cheated his way through medical school. No one wants to ride in an airplane designed by someone who cheated to get an engineering degree. No one wants to make investments based on financial reports prepared by someone who cheated to get an MBA.

Multiculturalism has failed. Multiculturalism was never the intention of our founding fathers. We need to return our culture to its Judeo-Christian roots. Values such as not stealing, not lying, not coveting, using a fair measure, and more are essential to the functioning of our schools, businesses, and government.

Chapter 9

Foreign Takeover of US Graduate

Schools

It's the fox watching the chicken house.

U S universities seek more of our taxes to fund research; however, the research they want funded is largely done by foreign graduate students and foreign born professors. *The media has done little to inform Americans of this dangerous foreign takeover.* [44]

Working on federally funded research educates the next generation of technology workers. [170] Such jobs should go to educate US citizens, not to educate people that may one day pose a threat to the US economically and/or militarily.

From 1985 through 1996, foreign students from China, India and Taiwan combined took *62% of the total science and engineering doctoral degrees awarded by US universities!* Universities in California awarded engineering degrees to Asians at more than *double the rate* of other US universities. [372]

In 2001, foreign students in our graduate schools took *60% of the computer engineering master's degrees, 69% of computer science master's degrees, and 52% of the dual computer science/engineering master's degrees.* [363] [226] [770]

Asians are more than 1500% overrepresented in our university high tech doctoral programs. These US doctoral programs are <u>*the prime source for producing our college professors who act as expert advisors to our government and business leaders.*</u>

What is Going On?

For a group that comprises about 3% of our population to take over half of the doctoral degrees in high tech US graduate school programs shows something is highly askew. Either Asians are racially superior, as some argue, or something very sinister is going on in our college admissions and financial aid.

The racial superiority argument is not credible given that the US for decades was technologically advanced far beyond China and India. In the 1970's when foreign students from Asia began to flood into US universities, we were the undisputed world leader in software and computer information systems. In contrast, both India and China were notorious for pirating our software and technology.

Why Our Universities Seek Foreign Graduate Students

Our universities made money educating foreign students to take Americans' jobs. The job turnover increased demand for classes. [224] [47] And, they cut costs by using H-1Bs to teach undergraduate classes.

Outsourcing firms also provided financial incentives to our universities. For example, one consulting company set up a program with the Dean of George Mason University that offered scholarships, housing, and paid internships for students from India. [256]

The biggest financial incentive came from our taxes funding research. According to Dr. Norman Matloff, the science and engineering reputation of a US university is based on how much research money it is awarded, particularly from the US government. *The research money is mostly used to pay graduate students to conduct research. To get the money, US universities need to get graduate students. Apparently there is no requirement that students doing sensitive government funded research are US citizens.* The US overproduced PhDs, yet universities increased recruiting to get more of our taxes to fund research. [186] We are caught in a self destructive cycle of funding a foreign takeover of our research.

Professors with Foreign Agendas

The demographics of our professors ought to match our citizens. However, because *most colleges require professors to have a PhD, the foreign takeover of our graduate schools paved the way for the foreign takeover of our universities.* US University faculty positions gave foreign born professors a platform for recruiting foreign students, and for creating studies to promote visa worker programs, and outsourcing.

When Americans protest "globalization" the mantra of the foreign born professors is, *"there is no turning back."* They want us to think that outsourcing cannot be stopped. When of course not only can it be stopped, it must be stopped. Globalization has enriched a few greedy men to the detriment of people around the world. It is destroying our children's future.

Professors with foreign agendas can stack the deck against young American students and American businesses. The grades and references they confer determine who is considered *the best and brightest* and who gets hired. They select students who work on our tax funded research projects, and *who is recognized for the patents awarded.* Most importantly, they select business partners that license our tax funded university patents for profit. [45]

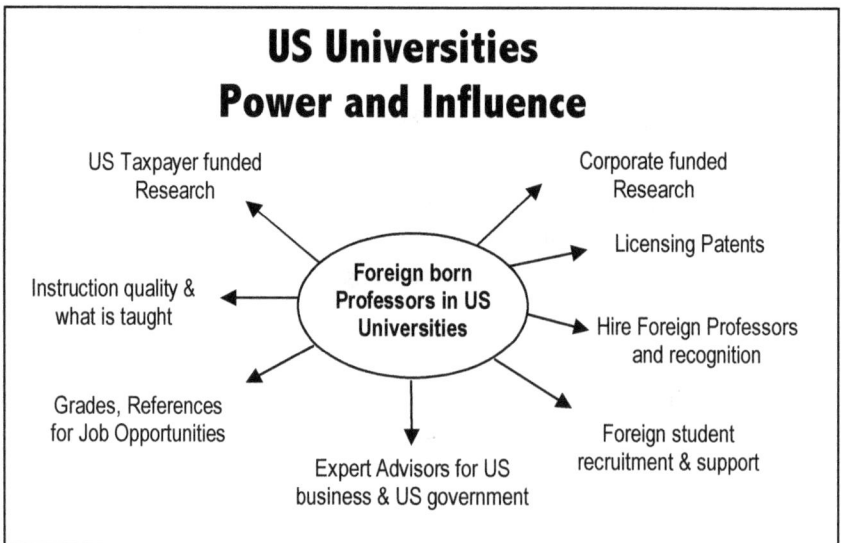

US Universities Power and Influence

US Taxpayer funded Research

Corporate funded Research

Licensing Patents

Instruction quality & what is taught

Foreign born Professors in US Universities

Hire Foreign Professors and recognition

Grades, References for Job Opportunities

Expert Advisors for US business & US government

Foreign student recruitment & support

Financial Aid Misappropriated

Some colleges took aid meant for American students and misdirected it to foreign students. For example, in 1997, our government was investigating allegations that *administrators at a college awarded grants to foreign students who were not qualified and redirected federal money meant for American students to foreign students instead.* [252]

Americans protested when our government was billed millions of dollars for foreign students' graduate school *tuition waivers to help foreign PhD students get jobs in university research programs.* [252] No wonder they outnumber Americans in our graduate schools.

Universities also misused alumni contributions and corporate matching funds to pay for foreign student *tuition, housing, H-1B visa workshops and even social networking activities.* Universities should be required to disclose to alumni how much money they channeled to foreign students.

In 2007, students from India arrived with almost no resources, yet they planned multi-year stays. So who was paying for their education? They came here for high tech training, *so that they could return to India to fill offshored American jobs.* About 450 were attending NC State. They kept a low profile and clustered together for living and socializing. There were so many that *one Indian said that he thought Americans felt out of place in NC State engineering classes.* [626]

Duke University is financially out of reach for most Americans. In 2008, a freshman from China with "*full financial aid*" admitted that it was, "*Not my academic records*" that got her into Duke. In a campus controversy over Tibet, "*she lectured Chinese students in English about being more tolerant and open to dialogue with the pro-Tibet side.*" However, she wrote in Chinese that she was against Tibet and: "*The Americans want to roast us in hot coals ... Be sure not to let them take advantage or show off their cleverness.*" [693] *Given our trade deficit why would a student from China get any aid, moreover if she is anti-American why were we educating her?* How many more students who are anti-American are being educated at our expense?

Many Students in Asia Get a Free Education

University students in India can focus on studies and not worry about college expenses. It costs about $3,000 per student per year to attend the Indian Institute of Technology (IIT) and the government of India picks up the tab. [303] India's diaspora living in the United States also funded educating students in India. The Chinese government paid to educate huge numbers of IT workers. [774]

Moreover, executives in US corporations used corporate money to fund educating foreign students in China and India in preparation for offshoring our jobs.

White Americans Discriminated Against

The *"traditional students"* (white) were discriminated against in US college admissions and financial aid in favor of *"non-traditional students"* (any race but white). Non-white foreign students studying in the US benefited from preferential financial aid treatment. Our government, foreign governments, and outsourcing companies subsidized their education.

Bottom line, the children of Americans were discriminated against, and foreign students were favored on our college campuses. Americans should not be discriminated against, because they have white skin. Our founding fathers were white. Globally whites are a minority. The descendents of the majority of American soldiers who fought and died for this country, and the scientists, inventors, farmers, teachers, and other Americans who built America are discriminated against in our universities. Can you imagine Chinese universities giving preferential admissions and financial support favoring non-Chinese students? Or, can you imagine Indian universities giving preferential admissions and financial support favoring non-Indians?

Do the demographics of the students that received NSF and other federal technology scholarships reflect the demographics of our overall population?

Dangerous Drop in American Enrollments

The 1990 H-1B legislation caused dramatic drops in the enrollments of Americans into engineering and computer science degree programs. The combination of high college costs, depressed wages and the lack of job opportunities discouraged young Americans from pursing technology degrees. The first big drop in undergraduate electronic engineering degrees occurred in 1995.

In 2001, we again experienced a steep decline in the number of Americans enrolling in computer science programs. The decline continued. A 2004 National Science Board (NSB) report found that *the US had dangerously dropped in the proportion of 18 to 24 year olds pursing degrees in engineering and natural science. While the US was 3rd in the world in 1975, by 2004 we had fallen to 17th.* [221] A 2004 study found that young Americans had the qualifications, but excessive costs, and perceived lack of job opportunities were the reason for the decline. [261]

In 2005, *over 400,000 American engineers were laid off, at the same time executives persuaded Congress to expand the H-1B program.* So it is no surprise we experienced more dramatic drops in the number of Americans enrolling in technology degree programs that year. *American students are too bright to pursue a degree in a profession where the wages have been depressed by foreign workers and executives are channeling the jobs to foreign graduate students.* [45] [250] [615] [255] [81]

In 2006, The Programmers Guild asked our government to increase US employers' H-1B fees to $5,000 per H-1B per year. The *fees would fund educating Americans in programming and engineering areas where companies claimed the US had shortages.* Industry lobbies objected saying that since the H-1B program began they had paid over $1 billion in H-1B fees to provide scholarships and training for Americans. However if it costs $60,000 for a four year degree, *$1 billion would have paid to educate less than 16,000 Americans during the 16 years of the H-1B program.* [741]

"Where are the Programmers?" a 2007 article warned few Americans were pursuing computer science studies at a time when we needed programmers for complex multi-core processors. [619]

Lowering Education Quality

Foreign graduate students often get jobs as teaching assistants. American college students complained that foreign graduate students provided poor quality instruction. Comparing test scores of students taught by foreign graduate assistants against those taught by US citizen professors supports their inferior instruction claims. [230] Recall many foreign students used fake credentials to get their visas so they would not be qualified to teach. Moreover, since the majority of foreign students planned to seek employment in the US in violation of their visas, *they had an inherent conflict of interest to be teaching the children of US citizens who they wanted to compete against in our job market.*

Disincentives for American to Pursue PhDs

There are three big disincentives for Americans to pursue PhDs doing research in our universities. *First, foreign students artificially depressed university research pay, so for Americans* doing research compared to getting a job in industry may not make financial sense. [186] Second, young Americans saddled with a huge undergraduate college debt, might be reluctant to go into more debt to attend graduate school. Finally, most companies do not offer better job opportunities to Americans with advanced degrees.

Demographics Should Mirror our Population

Bill Clinton said: "*Every single Palestinian I know in America is a millionaire or a college professor.*" [840] How many Palestinians are US college professors? The demographics of our professors and students should mirror our population.

The children of people who entered the US under the fraudulent H-1B and other visa programs should not be favored in US college admissions and financial aid over the children of the Americans who they unjustly displaced.

Chapter 10

Studies Mislead Congress

Prior to "globalization" university studies helped position us for success.

Now many studies are propaganda tools promoting visas, and outsourcing.

Our universities turned into propaganda machines when executives commissioned university studies to sell visa programs, outsourcing, and offshoring to our government. There was an *"understanding that the outcome of the studies will be in industry's favor."* [24]

"Studies" persuaded our Congress to pass the H-1B visa program and to increase visa caps. Universities receive industry research funding and cannot afford to alienate executives. Moreover, by supporting the claims of a high tech labor shortage, US universities could get more research money from Congress. They could flood graduate school programs with foreign students from China and India. [494]

A 2004 *economictimes.indiatimes.com* article, "US Professors: New Age Ambassadors for India Inc." said US professors from India were working with India's outsourcing firms to generate studies. Infosys and Wipro, wanted to keep it "under wraps" that they were working with US professors to develop pro-outsourcing case studies. Their goal was to *"strike the right balance"* in the outsourcing debate to, *"help the Indian IT industry, against the ever increasing backlash."* [245] So, these were not really studies. They were outsourcing marketing tools to benefit India parading under the guise of "studies."

Outsourcing "Studies" Full of Holes

It is difficult to find US university professors willing to criticize the H-1B visa program, outsourcing, and offshoring because of the lure of money and the threat of personal attacks. Nonetheless, here are three.

Outsourcing America a book by college professors Ron and Anil Hira, immigrants from India, poked holes in pro-outsourcing studies:

1)   They said the 2004 Global Insight Study done for ITAA was propaganda used to lobby for outsourcing.

2)   They criticized the Catherine Mann study as being overly optimistic, using flawed logic, and not understanding the strategic implications of outsourcing technology jobs.

3)   Finally, they dismissed the McKinsey study as a lobbying tool to help sell outsourcing. [81]

Another critic is Dr. Norman Matloff, a Professor in the Department of Computer Science at the University of California, Davis. In 1998, he testified to the US House Judiciary Committee Subcommittee on Immigration. His paper, "Debunking the Myth of a Desperate Software Labor Shortage," exposed that: *"These lobbyists know very well how to play the political game. They know, for example, that politicians like to use academic 'studies' for cover."* He explained: *"Industry lobbyists know that they can count on academia to produce seemingly unbiased studies which in fact are designed from the outset to produce results supportive of industry's position."* [24]

Dr. Matloff also wrote: *"Globalization and the American IT Worker: Exporting IT jobs and importing IT workers not only harms U.S. IT workers, it also harms U.S. firms and the broader economy."* [745] and *"Offshoring: What Can Go Wrong?" "Distance, cultural differences, inexperienced programmers, and other obstacles might make you wish you'd kept that IT project at home."* [746]

"Groundbreaking Study" or Propaganda?

AnnaLee Saxenian, Dean of the School of Information Management and Systems at the University of California Berkley, is *frequently quoted by people promoting student visas, H-1B visas, outsourcing, and offshoring.* For example, an article, "Where Integrated Chips Means Indians, Chinese," quoted Saxenian's *"groundbreaking study."* [330] The title of the article is erroneous, because neither Indians nor Chinese invented the integrated chip for computers.

Saxenian lauded H-1Bs as *"agents of global change"* who circulated US technology discoveries to India and China. Her May 2000, "Silicon Valley's New Immigrant Entrepreneurs" paper hyped the *"superior educational attainment"* of immigrants working in Silicon Valley. She said 55% of Indians, and 40% of Chinese held graduate degrees. In contrast she said *only 18% of their white counterparts held graduate degrees.* [372] She failed to acknowledge that these racial differences were because students from China and India used our graduate schools to bypass US immigration controls. And, that for most Americans advanced degrees rarely yielded better jobs.

She also credited these immigrants with the outsourcing of our jobs: "***The pool of people that came to the US and went to school and then ended up often in places like Silicon Valley has paved the way for this outsourcing***" Saxenian explained that *immigrants used their contacts and knowledge of Indian culture and institutions to establish the offshore outsourcing links between Silicon Valley in the US and India.* [379] So student visas are at the root cause of our job losses.

She claimed immigrant entrepreneurs created economic wealth. That must explain the record California budget surplus—oops deficit. And she claimed they created jobs. If they created 150,000 jobs in Silicon Valley from 1975 to 1990, and during that same time period the number of foreign-born workers doubled to 350,000, then they took more jobs than they created. [372]

Despite all her hype, an examination of the immigrant startups revealed that most did not create breakthrough leading edge technologies. [329]

According to her paper Satish Gupta claimed immigrants were successful because of *trust based on factors such as caste, mannerisms and culture.* [372] This discriminates against most Americans.

Where was Saxenian shortly after the dotcom crash that took our country into an economic nosedive? She was listed as a speaker for a 2000 *The IndUS Entrepreneurs* (TiE) Conference that was held in Bangalore, India. This conference celebrated the benefits of US outsourcing to India. (See also TiE "India Mafia")

In a 2002 article, Saxenian advocated open environments where information flows "*across traditional boundaries.*" [378] If she is advocating the flow of US technology secrets, that may involve breaking US intellectual property laws and may break other laws.

Opponents to the H-1B visas claimed Saxenian protested when the US Department of Defense attempted to prevent foreign nationals from working on sensitive US defense research. They said she warned that without foreign nationals, there would not be enough high tech workers to staff defense projects. She *asserted that every company in Silicon Valley had 10% to 40% foreign nationals as employees.* [389]

Saxenian, while advocating foreign access to sensitive defense technology, has also advised and/or provided input to multiple US government agencies including our National Academy of Sciences, and National Research Council and the National Science Foundation. [482]

A truly groundbreaking study would be one that exposed how foreign nationals penetrated so deeply into American defense contractors.

"Global Advantage" or Propaganda?

Vivek Wadhwa collaborated with Saxenian to produce his 2007 study, "America's New Immigrant Entrepreneurs." [685] The day his study was released *Indolink.com* declared his study *"confirms and extends the earlier findings by AnnaLee Saxenian"* that, *"first generation Indian-Americans have become a significant driving force in the creation of new businesses and intellectual property in the U.S. since 1990."* [685]

Wadhwa said the study was done because US competitiveness was threatened by a *"growing momentum of outsourcing critical research."* [685] Where was most of this research outsourced? To his native India.

Wadhwa and his masters degree students at Duke *decided to study the contributions of foreign students who stayed and worked in America.* Students doing the study were: *Ramakrishnan Balasubramanian, Pradeep Kamsali, Nishant Lingamneni, Niyanthi Reddy, and Batul Tambawalla,* [685]

Wadhwa *acknowledged that foreign students came from countries that were becoming a growing competitive threat to the United States.* Yet, he said granting them permanent status will *"likely lead to greater economic growth and create a greater intellectual property and competitive advantage."* [632]

However, to determine what is "likely" let's compare our competitive position prior to 1970 when they began to flood our universities. At that time neither India nor China posed any threat to US intellectual property leadership.

His study reported that *people from India founded more high tech companies in the US from 1995-2005, than immigrants from Britain, China, Taiwan and Japan all totaled.* *Indian startups were concentrated in software and services for manufacturing and research.* [632] He said earlier studies focused on *"contributions"* of immigrants who founded dotcoms. [687]

- *Wadhwa himself founded two startups. He was one of the first CEOs to hire H-1Bs.* [780] [685] *An article, "Indian Owns a Goldmine," said his company Relativity made millions transferring US citizens' credit histories, insurance claims, medical data, and property records to the Internet. His competitor, Tibco, was also founded by an Indian immigrant.* [688] *Putting this data on the Internet enabled offshoring.*

Wadhwa's study claimed that non-citizens (*foreign graduate students, green card holders, and visa workers*) were named as inventors or co-inventors on 24.2% of the 2006 US international patent applications. He said this was impressive since people from India and China make up *less than 1% of the population in the US.* [632] However, he's not using the most relevant percentage. Students from China and India take about 50% of the seats in our university research labs. So, filing *for 24.2% of the patent applications would not be impressive.*

Moreover, a patent application does not mean a patent will be awarded. Besides, patents are not a numbers game. *One really significant patent may be more valuable than thousands of others.* The biggest factor skewing the patent application statistics was because <u>millions of highly skilled American programmers, scientists and engineers were displaced by foreign visa workers. This dramatically decreased the number of Americans working on research and filing patents.</u>

Wadhwa concluded: *"After analyzing the data, my view is that America doesn't need more temporary workers it needs more immigrants."* [685] His study *"received worldwide attention and acclaim."* [685] Is anyone surprised that people who want to immigrate to our country praised a study that claimed we need more immigration? [685] [632]

Critics of H-1B visas had trouble getting media coverage. Yet, Wadhwa was *"featured in thousands of articles ... including The Wall Street Journal, Forbes Magazine, Washington Post, New York Times, U.S. News and World Report and Science Magazine."* He was on ABC, NBC, CNBC, CNN, and BBC. [686] Where is fair and balanced coverage in our media?

In an *EETimes* 2007 article, "Green-card Red Tape Sends Valuable Engineers Packing," Wadhwa said that *500,000 foreign visa holders were in line for green cards,* but only 120,000 per year were available. He warned that if they do not get green cards: *"they become our competitors. That's as stupid as it gets. ... <u>How can this country be so dumb as to bring people in on temporary visas, train them in our way of doing business and then send them back to compete with us?</u>"* [703] That is a very good question.

Global IT ACM Study

The 83,000 member Association for Computing Machinery did an IT outsourcing study and emphasized that its report was not from a "*United States-centric perspective.*" [557] Rather, its goal was to study globalization of our software industry. *The study found that most of the growth in offshoring had occurred in "the past five years,*" i.e. *following the US dotcom crash.* And, it acknowledged that globalization created national security risks for the US and jeopardized our technology leadership. Yet, it concluded that these risks would not slow offshoring.

The study reported that *education was the key enabler of offshoring to countries such as India and China.* Curiously, the study then claimed we needed to recruit and educate more foreign students. ACM recommended: "*eliminate barriers to the free flow of talent.*" [557]

This study predicted that *IT jobs would be among the highest growth jobs for the next decade, and that 12-14 million more US jobs were targeted for offshoring over a 15 year period.* Venture capital companies were forcing offshoring of R&D by requiring *as a condition for funding, that US startups use offshore workers* to reduce the "*burn rate*" of money invested. The report downplayed high tech American job losses claiming the losses were small compared to the yearly job loss/job creation cycle in the US. The study *used the US economic downturn caused by the dotcom crash to justify offshoring.* [557]

Contrived Studies Accountability

If you think about it, we are paying record levels of tuition and taxes to fund universities that promote outsourcing and offshoring our jobs. How smart can these 'experts' be if they are cutting the source of income for the people they depend on to survive? Of course, what they should be teaching is critical thinking that exposes the risks and long term implications to our nation and future. We need to make sure that studies our Congress and business leaders rely on tell both sides, and are not compromised by conflicts of interests.

Chapter 11

"Management Thinkers from

India"

Pre-globalization: "Our employees are our most valuable resource."

The New Mantra: US employees are our most expendable resource.

Americans business management strategists made ours the most prosperous nation in the world. [372] At the very foundation of their advice was the core premise that *"our employees are our most valuable resource."*

Then our business leaders were led down the path by a new mantra *"our employees are our most expendable resource."* Management thinkers from India advised Corporate American executives that offshoring to India was essential to maintain competitive advantage because programmers in India were paid *"only 15%-20%"* of what US programmers were paid. By 1997, India was producing *"about 80,000-85,000 software professionals per year."* [335]

Common sense would tell you that transferring strategic US high tech jobs to India would jeopardize our competitive advantage, not help us retain it. This was done *"quietly."* Most of these "management thinkers" advising executives kept a low profile because they did not want you to know who they are and what role they played.

Thinkers "Changing the Face of American Business"

"The Indians are Coming—How <u>Management Thinkers from India</u> are Changing the Face of American Business," a 2005 article provided insight into their goal of *"changing the face of American business."* Most if not all of these "thinkers" came to the US on *student visas with our financial aid.* Several attended Harvard. Instead of returning to India, they sought jobs as professors and advisors. Armed with Masters degrees and PhDs from our universities, they marketed themselves as *"management thinkers," "superstars," "strategy gurus," "executive coaches."* [240]

We revere our universities as sources of expert knowledge. *These "thinkers" used their affiliation and credentials with our universities to get articles and books promoting visas, outsourcing and offshoring published.* Many of our businesses were lured into offshoring by "globalization" propaganda these immigrants spun to benefit India. They advised that people who *"invest their human capital in the company, will expect a return on it, and expect growth of that capital."* [240] This was the same as *"our employees are our most valuable resource."* Yet, they persuaded executives to break the social contract with Americans who invested their *"human capital"* and made our nation the world leader.

The article revealed the disturbing secret of their success: *"<u>India's collectivist culture offers a ready foil to America's rampant individualism.</u>"* [240] They acted as a collective not individually in business dealings. They unwisely used Enron as an example to berate American individualism. Enron was a poor choice, because it was a collective deception by co-conspirators. And, because part of the Enron deception involved using millions of our tax dollars to fund building a power plant in India for which we were not repaid.

"While no one can predict the Indian thinkers' long term impact on American businesses, there is no question that they are bringing refreshing diversity to boardrooms and MBA programs," the article said. [240] To the contrary, their impact is obvious in our trade deficit, and high unemployment.

Who Are Some of These "Management Thinkers"?

Who are some of these *"management thinkers from India"* promoting outsourcing and offshoring to India? Well, there is Ram Charan [240] an *"executive coach"* to GE's Jack Welch who was nicknamed "Neutron Jack" because he laid off so many Americans when he offshored work to India. [66] A few more of *"management thinkers from India:"*

UNIVERSITY OF MICHIGAN PROFESSORS—CK PRAHALAD & M.S. KRISHNAN

C.K. Prahalad, born in India, became a US citizen and a professor at the University of Michigan. [240] He worked as a *"business consultant"* promoting outsourcing and offshoring to India. Prahalad *said that people were caught off guard by "the rate at which China and India are acquiring a world-class technology base and the speed at which they are beating others."* [253] Prahalad appeared in a 2006 ABC News piece that promoted India as *"the destination for American business outsourcing."* [513] Note: they were "acquiring" our technology.

M.S. Krishnan graduated from the University of Delhi in India. He obtained a Masters degree in 1993, and a PhD in 1996 from Carnegie Mellon. M.S. Krishnan became a professor at the University of Michigan. He is *on the boards of multiple academic journals* and has published about 40 articles. [649] He said: *"If you look at globalization the wheel is not going to stop. ... If U.S. companies compete globally, it's unavoidable that they will have manufacturing in China and Taiwan, design and software in India, probably marketing and strategy in the United States. ..."* [253] Krishnan may be surprised at how quickly Americans can stop the *"globalization wheel."* We successfully competed globally for many years without offshoring to China or India.

In 2004, together Prahalad and Krishnan persuaded the University of Michigan to set up a research center at IIT in Bangalore, India. Their plan was to arrange for US faculty and students to take trips to India and work on research projects. Did US taxpayers and/or US students' tuition fund this research center?

VIJAY GOVINDARAJAN—TUCK UNIVERSITY PROFESSOR

Vijay Govindarajan was born in India. He entered the US as a student to attend Harvard. [240] Around 1985, he became the first person from India to obtain a faculty position at Tuck University.

Govindarajan used his US professor credentials to help him become *one of the highest paid executive coaches in Corporate America*. [240] US Executives may have been less receptive to his "advice" if they knew he said, *"the center of gravity cannot simply be the United States."* He admitted that by persuading companies to offshore to India he was personally profiting, *"my market value is going up."* [240]

He took 50 young American executives on a trip to India. One asked an Infosys executive if he was concerned IBM or Accenture may try to acquire Infosys. *Govindarajan proudly recalled the Indian executive responded that maybe Infosys might acquire IBM or Accenture.* [240]

Govindarajan claimed, *"there is no doubt that Indians have had a disproportionate influence on management thinking and practice. As a percentage of the U.S. population, they are miniscule—less that a single percent—but then look at their representation in business schools."* [240] In 2005 he boasted that 20% of the faculty at Tuck originated from India, and 40 students from India entered Tuck's MBA program. *There is something disturbing about a group that comprises less than a "single percent" of the US demographically controlling 20% of the teaching positions in a US university*, especially since they recruit foreign students from India.

How brilliant is Govindarajan to be so highly paid? He argued that 20% of people are smart; so India has 200 million smart people. [240] If his logic that a bigger population creates more smart people is true, then India would have been more prosperous than the US. The truth is overpopulation drains scarce resources, which in turn interferes with a nation being able to focus on R&D and provide quality education. India had more people than the US in the 1950's-1970's yet India was not even close to our nation's success.

Mohanbir Sawhney—"My Scam"

Mohanbir Sawhney got a Ph.D. from the Wharton. [235] He then he became a professor at Northwestern's Kellogg School. [240] Sawhney used his professorship to become an *advisor to CEOs of big US corporations.* [191] He also co-founded a consulting company for startups that he claimed, *"pretty much locked up the Chicago-area deal flow."* Sawheny was on the board for 5 startups and on 16 advisory boards preparing for IPOs at the peak of the dotcom boom. *He did not invest in the startups, yet he demanded 1% equity or more for his help.* He called himself a "market maker" and jokingly called it *"my scam."* [237]

"Professors Profiting from Practicing What They Teach," a 2000 article said it is common for professors to do consulting and serve as experts on corporate boards. However, *it saw serious issues in the case of startup ventures where professors leveraged their university connections to become millionaires.* [238] One of the professors named was Sawhney. In January 2001 Sawhney resigned as a high profile board member of Divine interVentures after its stock plunged to about $1 per share. [236]

A partial list of companies Sawhney advised: outsourcing-Accenture, Infosys (India), and IBM; *financial*-Bank of America and Goldman Sachs; *software*-Adobe and Microsoft; *technology*-Boeing, Cisco, Dell, Motorola, Rockwell, Dow Chemical, DuPont, Ericsson, Honeywell; and more. [235] *Honeywell offshored jobs to 95 countries.* [108]

Sawhney told Boeing executives in 2003, *"that the company had a long way to go before it can consider itself a truly global company."* [239] Boeing outsourced development to *"partners around the world,"* expecting to cut costs $10 billion. The production of its 787 was to *"revolutionize the way Boeing manufactures planes."* However in 2007, Boeing was *"facing the gloomy prospect of shelling out millions of dollars in penalties"* due to delays. Ann All's, post on *ITBusinessEdge* observed: *"Boeing's problems are a testament to the risks and limitations of outsourcing and global supply chains."* [670] In 2005 *BusinessWeek* still touted Sawhney as one of the 25 most influential people in e-Business. [235]

Rajat Gupta– McKinsey & Co. and Pan IIT

As mentioned earlier, Rajat Gupta as Managing Director of McKinsey & Co. claimed offshoring to India benefited Americans. [300] [334] [187] Critics wrote two books about McKinsey–*The Witch Doctors*, and *Dangerous Company: The Consulting Powerhouses and the Businesses They Save and Ruin.* [696] McKinsey teamed up with NASSCOM, India's powerful software lobby. [100] "Making of a Software Superpower," a 1999 article, said "*NASSCOM has played a key role in propagating India as the destination for software services and development.*" [228] A NASSCOM-McKinsey "study" predicted India's IT industry would *jump from $3 billion in 1998 to $90 billion by 2008.* [176] [124] A 30 fold increase!

NASSCOM commissioned another McKinsey Global "study" to argue offshoring was good for our economy. IBM used this report to justify its offshoring plans. [100] "India: IT Outsourcing Aids U.S. Other Economies," a 2003 *asia.cnet.com* story said NASSCOM claimed that *American banks, financial services companies, and insurance companies saved $6-$8 billion over the last four years due to outsourcing IT to India.* [67]

A "Technology Without Borders Global iit2005 Conference," co-chaired by Rajat Gupta, encouraged IIT Alumni to network to *find business partners, obtain access to US university research, obtain subcontracts from our government, and to lend a hand to India's government.* [523] This conference proudly displayed *House Resolution 227* where our Congress formally recognized *India's Indian Institute of Technology (IIT)*, and called for Americans to appreciate IIT graduates' contributions. How could our Congress call for Americans to appreciate losing millions of jobs to foreign visa workers, outsourcing and offshoring? *Bobby Jindal and Tom Davis co-sponsored this resolution in 2005.*

Conference speaker Hiten Ghosh, told about a 2002 meeting in McKinsey's Connecticut offices where 50 IIT graduates *hatched the idea to promote "brand IIT" as a "household name in USA"* because–"*in the USA, increased globalization is threatening decades of high living standards.*"

They formed *Pan-IIT, a non-profit US corporation umbrella organization in response to* India's Prime Minister Jawharlal Nehru's call for "*Service to the nation*" to transform India by "*Giving Back.*"

They were expected to link IITs to *US research universities.* By the time of the Conference *Pan-IIT had 12 Chapters in North America.* [523] The first Pan-IIT conference in 2002 was held in Washington, DC, later meetings alternated "*between the United States and India.*"

They were pleased with the "*excellent media coverage.*" *BusinessWeek* and Cartoons such as Dilbert were used to promote "brand IIT." And, CBS's "*60 Minutes*" promoted IIT as a "*world-class brand.*" [523] [523]

FOREIGN EXCHANGE ZAKARIA INTERVIEWED GUPTA

"Sizing Up the Competition" a 2007 PBS "Foreign Exchange with Fareed Zakaria," show featured an interview with *Rajat Gupta, former head of McKinsey, and current Chairman of Pan IIT Global.* [640] They revealed 50,000 IIT graduates were in the US. Gupta said IIT graduates "*tremendously contributed to this (United States) economy, and created a tremendous number of jobs.*" He claimed IIT graduates formed "*the backbone of the tech industry*" in America. [640] However, America was the world technology leader well before any IIT graduates came here to be educated in our graduate schools.

Zakaria called India's IIT the "*MIT of the East.*" He wondered how India was able to fund IIT because of the poverty (apparently he does not know US aid helped fund IIT). Zakaria asked if *it's a waste of money to educate American scientists when India can produce scientists cheaper.*

Gupta talked about the *outsourcing "revolution" that used* globalization to break down barriers to US jobs. He told how 15 years earlier he used consulting to sway American companies to offshore research to India. *Zakaria asked if America had only seen the "tip of the iceberg with outsourcing?" And Gupta responded, "Yeah."* [640] (In 2012, Zakaria who came to the US on a scholarship in 1982, was charged with plagiarism and briefly suspended from his CNN post, and Gupta was found guilty of insider trading.)

Chapter 12

Exposing the Real Reasons

Behind the H-1B

When did "temporary" become synonymous with "permanent"?

There was no worker shortage, the "best and brightest" claims do not hold up, and the Economic Circulation Model™ disproves cost savings claims. So what was the truth?

The H-1B was not driven by any need the United States had, but rather by foreign nations that wanted access to strategic US technologies; and, by foreign students and illegal aliens who wanted high tech American jobs.

The stage was set for the foreign run on US jobs, when our government granted more than 3 million foreign student visas from 1971 - 1991. Even though they signed agreements that they would not attempt to stay in the US, 393,000 obtained green cards and most of the remaining 87% stayed illegally. [230]

This glut of illegal US college educated foreign workers tempted unscrupulous executives in US corporations to inflate earnings in the short term by replacing Americans with cheaper foreign workers.

These foreign students who stayed illegally were the ones who "paved the way" for outsourcing our jobs. They were behind the scenes in the shadows driving the H-1B bill scam. Accounting tricks linking H-1Bs to huge executive bonuses was their lure. Had our government done its job and enforced our immigration laws we would not be in a financial crisis.

H-1Bs Legalized Hiring Foreign Students

When you put side by side the growth in foreign student visas and the H-1B visas it all becomes clear. *The H-1B legislation was sought to legalize hiring foreigners educated in the US.* It is striking how the increases track. For example, by 1998 about six million foreign students had been awarded visas, allowing two to four years to graduate; you can see that by the year 2000 almost six million high tech work visas.

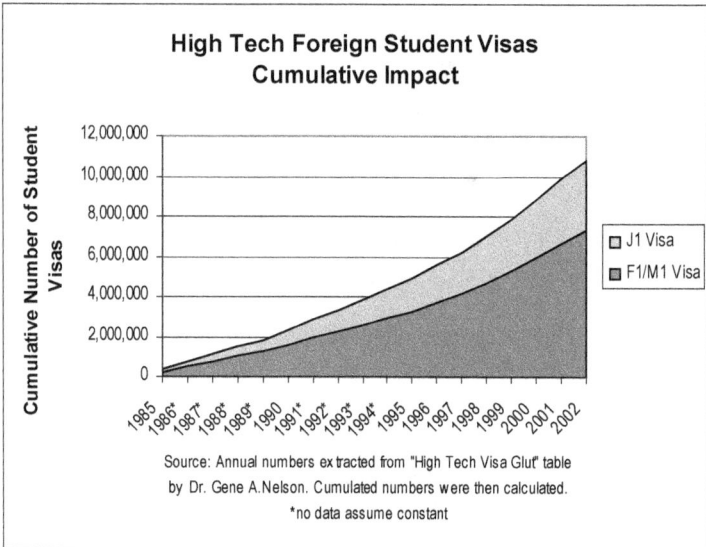

High Tech Foreign Student Visas Cumulative Impact

Source: Annual numbers extracted from "High Tech Visa Glut" table by Dr. Gene A. Nelson. Cumulated numbers were then calculated.
*no data assume constant

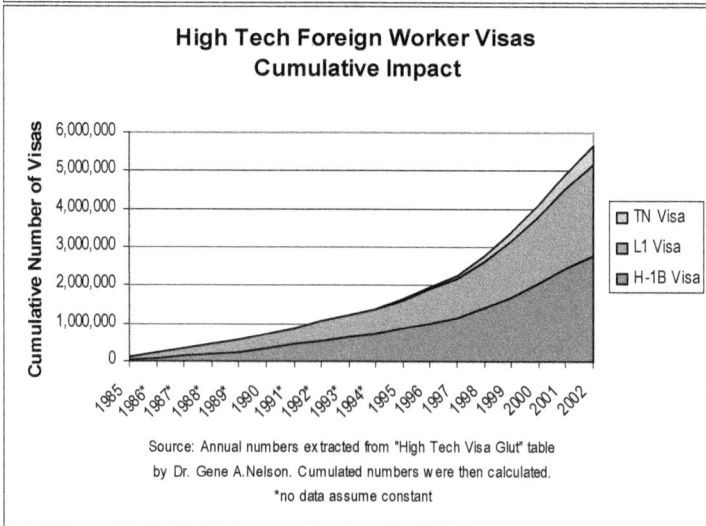

High Tech Foreign Worker Visas Cumulative Impact

Source: Annual numbers extracted from "High Tech Visa Glut" table by Dr. Gene A. Nelson. Cumulated numbers were then calculated.
*no data assume constant

Illegal Aliens Got H-1B Visas!

In 1996, there were so many visa violators in our country that *a law was passed requiring the INS to track visa holders.* By 2003 the INS had spent $31.2 million to build a computer system to track visa holders and identify violators. Yet, the system was not ready. The INS wanted *$57 million more to continue development.* [143] Were visa holders programming the system that would track them? Americans would have a strong incentive to protect their jobs—it is hard to imagine they would not have gotten this system up and running in 1996, much less *7 years later in 2003.*

Surprisingly, student visa violators who broke our immigration laws were not screened out when applying for H-1B visas. They got sensitive jobs in our government, universities, banks, accounting firms, and high tech US companies. In 2000, an estimated 53,300 foreigners already living in the US received 40% of the H-1Bs. A little more than half went to foreign students; many visas went to illegal aliens primarily from India, China, and the Middle East.

Executives Treated H-1Bs like Indentured Servants

Why did executives prefer hiring H-1Bs? H-1Bs were bound by restrictive work contracts. Executives misused these contracts to treat H-1Bs like indentured servants that they could overwork and underpay. If H-1Bs complained they could threaten to send them back to their country. In December 2000, an H-1B programmer from India complained that their status was like a *"modern-day slave."* [26]

One article reported that by using various schemes, executives were able to pay H-1Bs about a half of what they paid US citizens. [63] Other reports estimated that H-1Bs were paid 15% to 33% below normal or about $20,000 to $25,000 less. [34]

An Indian manager who had a green card helped companies hire H-1Bs, and explained that companies liked hiring H-1Bs, because they would work for low pay and put in fourteen hour days and not charge for overtime. [31]

India Drove H-1B Legislation

The majority of H-1Bs were computer programmers. *Almost 74% of the computer related H-1B jobs went to people from India.* [41] In 2000, the government of India lobbied to increase the H-1B visa program, so that they could "export" more Indians to the US. At that time the IT jobs offshored to India were lower skilled jobs. *India saw H-1Bs and L-1s taking our high tech jobs in the US as positioning to later move our high tech jobs offshore to India.* [30]

'Transferring' US High Tech Jobs to
Foreign Workers and Foreign Countries

| Foreign H-1B Visa Workers in United States | H-1B Conduit for offshore outsourcing | Foreign Workers in Foreign Country |

In 2005, using the World Trade Organization, the Indian government lobbied to eliminate the H-1B cap, and eliminate the requirement to pay H-1Bs the prevailing wage. [615]

Fudging the Numbers

"Tech Worker Group Files Complaints Over H-1B Job Ads" reported in 2006 The Programmers Guild was filing legal complaints because *ads to hire H-1Bs violated the U.S. Immigration and Nationality Act that requires jobs in the US must be available to citizens.* [594]

John Miano who has fought against H-1B fraud for many years wrote a 2011 article, "When in Doubt, Make It Up," where he investigated claims that only 43% of H-1B applications were approved in 2008. He looked the data up on a government website and found that the actual numbers showed 89% of the visas were approved that year. [949]

Chapter 13

H-1B Quota Increases & Exemptions

From Bad to Worse.

Not only did Congress pass the original H-1B bill in 1990, it repeatedly compounded the harm to American workers by raising the annual H-1B visa quota caps and allowing exemptions.

A Senator from Utah exposed how executives got Congress to pass H-1B quota increases: *"There were in fact, a whole lot of folks against it, but because they are tapping the high-tech community for campaign contributions, they don't want to admit that in public."* [24]

1998 H-1B Quota Increased to 115,000

Senator Spencer Abraham sponsored a bill to increase the H-1B quota in February 1998. The White House Office of Management and Budget criticized his bill for focusing on providing job opportunities for foreign workers and failing to protect and provide work opportunities for US citizens. [12] [13]

Executives from major US corporations, including a VP from Sun, a VP from Microsoft, and the President and CEO of Cypress Semiconductor testified to Congress that the H-1B quota increase was essential *to fill worker shortages, and to protect US leadership in the computer industry.* [123] [13] [54]

Dr. Norman Matloff presented his study "Debunking the Myth of a Desperate Software Labor Shortage" to the U.S House Judiciary Committee's Subcommittee on Immigration in April 1998. He found the claims of US worker shortages were false. [24] His findings were supported by a 1998 IEEE-USA/Harris Poll that found 82% of US citizens did not believe we had a high tech worker shortage. [36]

To overcome opposition, Silicon Valley executives engaged in intense lobbying. The TechNet PAC hosted more than 70 meetings and *fundraisers*, and met with our President, Vice President, Speaker, House Representatives and Senate leaders.

Sponsoring the H-1B quota increase paid off for Abraham. Even though he wasn't up for reelection for 2 years, *executives at Syntel, Mastech, Sun Microsystems, Microsoft, and the American Immigration Lawyers Association (AILA) all made advance donations to his campaign fund.* [22] [468]

■　　*While a US Senator from 1995-2001, Abraham chaired the Senate Immigration Committee, and the Manufacturing Competitiveness Committee, and wrote the "H-1B Visa in Global and National Commerce Act."* [517]

Despite strong opposition, Congress stealthily passed his 1998 H-1B visa quota increase, *"but only when hidden within the budget bill."* [46]

At first the Clinton administration opposed increasing the H-1B cap. [13] However, *later President Clinton did a flip flop and signed. The 1998 law increased the H-1B quota limit to 115,000 visas per year.* After signing, Clinton *"went on a major fundraising tour of Silicon Valley and some other high-tech regions."* [24]

H-1Bs Hired May 1998 to July 1999
INS February 2000 Report
[41]

All Other 43%

India 48%

China 9%

Clinton Delivered the Mother Load for India

Clinton talks about all the jobs he created as President. How many of these jobs went to H-1Bs? A March 2000 article in Bombay India: "India's High-Tech Hopes" extolled how Clinton's visit to India was an opportunity to increase H-1B quotas. [288]

Despite warnings of fraud and strong American opposition, Senators voted 95 to 1 to increase H-1B quotas. [26] The House wanted to add protections for American workers. Appallingly, after announcing there would be no vote that day–*when only 40 out of 435 representatives remained, they stealthily voted to approve the quota increase without adding protections*. [24] A Virginia Rep said: "*This is not a popular bill with the public. It's popular with the CEOs ... This is a very important issue for the high-tech executives who give the money.*" [24]

A few weeks later, Clinton hosted a "*mother of all official state banquets*" in honor of India's visiting Prime Minister. According to *indiatimes.com*, "Washington Largest Gathering of Indian Americans at State Banquet," almost 700 guests attended. They claimed it was the most lavish state dinner hosted by Clinton during his presidency. [281] How many attendees were outsourcing or offshoring our jobs?

"*In one of his last acts as President, Bill Clinton passed the American Competitiveness in the Twenty-First Century Act.*" This act increased H-1B quotas to 195,000. So under Clinton's watch *H-1B quotas tripled*. [42] But that's only half the picture. The bill he signed added quota exemptions for *H-1Bs in our universities, government labs, and H-1Bs employed by non-profits*. [42] Exemptions *allowed H-1Bs to take more than double the quota*.

Also, in 2000, "errors" in a computer program let thousands more H-1Bs into the US than the law allowed. The INS hired KPMG Peat Marwick as an outside auditor to find these H-1B *errors even though KPMG was a major employer of H-1Bs*. [27] The audit found over *22,000 excess visas were illegally granted*. [34] What was done? The INS overlooked the excess, and 22,000 more Americans lost their jobs.

Bill to End H-1B Blocked

H-1Bs were *"not supposed to be able to dislocate any American worker,"* Representative Tom Tancredo emphasized. He said the 90 day rule between the layoffs and hiring of H-1Bs should be extended to six months. [603]

"H-1B Visas—A Time to Cut Back," an article Tancredo wrote in 2002 *claimed that the INS concealed the number of exempted H-1B visas it issued.* [29] He cited a study that found *45% of the work experience claims on H-1B applications from India were fraudulent,* and that H-1Bs stayed in the US illegally after they lost their jobs. Consequently, he submitted bill H.R. 2688 to repeal the H-1B program *saying Congress is obligated to tell Americans the truth and that the need for H-1B workers was based on lies.* [603]

The US India Political Action Committee (USINPAC) claimed that it blocked Tancredo's bill to end the H-1B program.

Our government failed to adequately track the H-1B visas it granted, so there are wide variations in estimates. For example a report, "Amazing Facts and Statistics: Non-immigrant Foreign Work Visa Programs and Workers," *claimed over 4 million H-1B visas were granted from 1998 to 2001.* [28] In contrast, Tancredo reported about *1.4 million H-1B Visas were granted from 1998 to 2002.*

Why so much variability? Some counts may only include programmers and not engineers, accountants, medical workers, and others. Also, note the H-1B legislation was passed in 1990, so the first eight years of the program are not included in either of these estimates. [603]

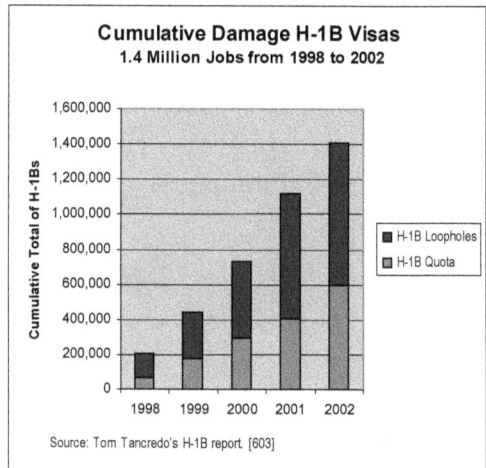

Cumulative Damage H-1B Visas
1.4 Million Jobs from 1998 to 2002

Cumulative Total of H-1Bs

1,600,000
1,400,000
1,200,000
1,000,000
800,000
600,000
400,000
200,000
0

1998 1999 2000 2001 2002

■ H-1B Loopholes
□ H-1B Quota

Source: Tom Tancredo's H-1B report. [603]

No Limit Exemptions & More Exemptions

Congress put <u>no limits on H-1Bs universities could hire</u> reported a 2002 *AsianWeek.com* article, "H-1B Visa Demand Rises." [40]

- *The top ten US universities hiring H-1Bs in 2006 included: University of Michigan, University of Illinois, University of Pennsylvania, John Hopkins University, University of Maryland, Columbia University, Yale, Harvard, Stanford and University of Pittsburg.* [665]

<u>*The INS acknowledged that the number of H-1B visas issued were more than double its official count in 2003.*</u> The INS also did not count H-1Bs who got extensions, nor the H-1Bs issued to universities and to non-profits because they are exempt from the quota controls. [63]

When the H-1B visa cap reverted back to 65,000 in 2004, it did little to help unemployed Americans because of *visa extensions, quota exemptions, alternate visas, and the acceleration of offshoring.*

Americans asked Congress to reform or end the H-1B in 2005. ITAA fought against requiring companies to prove they did not displace Americans, and tried to hire Americans. ITAA was pleased when President *Bush approved* <u>20,000 new exemptions</u> *to the H-1B cap* for foreign graduate students. *ITAA claimed that* <u>sending foreign students home would deprive America of its public investment in educating them.</u> [65]

H-1B Time Extensions

In 2002, the House voted 400 to 22 to approve H.R. 2215, a bill that allowed H-1Bs to <u>stay beyond the six year limit</u>, and it allowed medical students to stay in the US if they set up practice in rural communities. George W. Bush signed this bill. [60]

Microsoft praised US Homeland Security in 2008 for increasing the time foreign graduates could stay and search for US jobs to almost two and a half years! [727]

The INS has a mandate to deport H-1Bs if they are laid off or fired. Yet the INS informed H-1Bs that they would not be deported and that they could stay in the US to look for jobs. [28]

H-1B Expansion

"Congress Considers Massive H-1B Visa Expansion, Gates Tells Congress It's Microsoft's Top Priority," a 2006 article reported an attempt to grant 600,000 H-1Bs! Senator Arlen Specter drafted the immigration "reform" bill. Skeptics observed that if a shortage existed, Microsoft wages would have been growing, instead they had been mostly *"stagnate for several years."* [565]

■   *The top ten US technology companies that hired H-1Bs in 2006 listed in order included: <u>Microsoft</u>, IBM, Oracle Corporation, Cisco, Intel, Motorola, Qualcomm, Yahoo, HP and Google.* [665] *A few years later many of these companies were doing mass layoffs of Americans.*

Congress Passed More Foreign Worker Visa Programs

You should also know that large outsourcing firms hit the jackpot when Congress passed the L-1 visa. A 2006, article in India, "Worried about H-1B visa? Take the L1 Route," declared that President Bush's trip to India was *"a shot in the arm for Indians aspiring to work in America."* Because the <u>L-1 visa had no cap and could be used to get around H-1B limits</u>, and did not require paying the prevailing wage. [567] Congress also approved a TN visa similar to the H-1B for Canadians and Mexicans.

Congress passed the Trade Promotion Authority (TPA) in 2002, previously known as Fast Track. The TPA was sought by foreign nations who *"<u>do not have goods to trade, but they do have vast supplies of labor</u>."* To open up their markets to US companies these nations required that foreign workers could enter the US without immigration reviews. [60] TPA agreements put overpopulated countries in a position to overrun the US. Supposedly, a *TPA agreement cannot be repealed by the US Congress without the consent of the foreign country benefiting from the agreement.* [60]

Quota caps were becoming less relevant as companies and foreign countries accelerated offshoring our jobs.

Chapter 14

Outsourcing & Offshoring

Deceptions

Outsourcing was used to cover up displacing Americans with foreign workers.

Outsourcing occurs when a corporation contracts with an outsourcing company to do work that otherwise would have been done internally by full time employees. It was originally used to help companies with tasks that were outside the scope of their primary business. For example, a manufacturing company may outsource creating and maintaining employee handbooks to a company that specializes in writing handbooks. This type of limited outsourcing may be very beneficial. Most importantly it does not require the company to disclose any confidential information.

However, outsourcing took a twisted and sinister turn when it was exploited to displace college educated American programmers, engineers, accountants and more with foreign workers.

The whole concept of outsourcing our professional jobs to foreign workers was conflicted. Both the buyer (executives getting bonuses) and the seller (outsourcing company executives) had strong personal financial motivations that worked against you and other American workers.

How the Stage Was Set for Outsourcing our Jobs

First, let's look at how the stage was set for a mass "transfer" of our high tech jobs to foreign workers. Back in the late 70's and early 80's some US companies hired programmers and engineers as independent contractors. Because of the amount of time they were working, they should have been hired as fulltime employees with full benefits. So *to end the abuse, Congress passed the Tax Reform Act of 1986* which required that these independent contractors, be classified as fulltime employees.

Instead of the desired result, *large consulting companies sprang up that used outsourcing contracts to lock up the hiring for outsourced high tech jobs.* For Americans, the 1986 law made their situation far worse. To get work they had to become employees of outsourcing firms that paid low wages, required long hours, and provided fewer benefits than most US employers. [63] *Was there a hidden link to the 1986 amnesty and the birth of these outsourcing companies the same year?*

Outsourcing Dirty Secrets

The H-1B visa legislation passed in 1990 was a windfall for outsourcing companies. They gave polished presentations claiming they cut costs because of their methodologies. However, the truth was that many outsourcing companies, American owned and foreign owned, underhandedly cut costs by displacing Americans with foreign workers. *They became adept at making unqualified H-1Bs look highly skilled.* Americans were forced to write step-by-step guides. If an H-1B couldn't do the job, other employees in the consulting firm helped them look good. It is like having a whole network of people secretly helping you take a test. In school taking credit for work done by others would be called cheating.

Outsourcing companies can secretly sell the same work to a competitor. Imagine how impressed the next company will be when an unqualified H-1B simply keys in code, which may have been written originally by an American programmer.

Outsourcing Cover-up of Hiring Foreign Workers

When corporations hired visa workers and laid off Americans they were met with public protests and lawsuits. So, instead of hiring H-1Bs and L1s directly, executives used outsourcing to cover up job transfers to foreign workers. For example, when Americans laid off by Siemens were replaced with L-1 visa workers from Tata Consultancy, Americans protested. Siemens management responded, *"They don't work for us. They work for Tata."* [63] The *"thought leaders"* behind the transfer of our jobs to foreign workers make fun of you if you confuse outsourcing with hiring foreign workers directly.

When a company hires foreign workers directly, either in US or in a foreign country, the foreign workers become employees of the company. In this case Americans did not lose their job because of outsourcing. They lost their jobs because executives hired foreign employees to replace them.

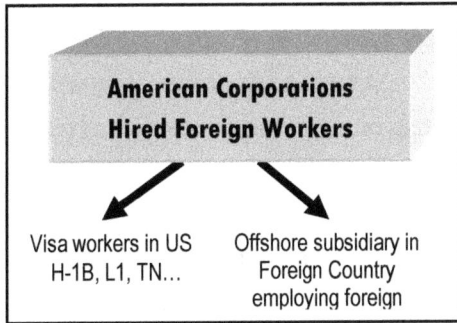

Outsourcing occurs when a company contracts with an outsourcing firm. The outsourced work may be done on the client's site, or at the outsourcing company's site. *The key difference is that the workers provided by the outsourcing company are employees of the outsourcing company, not employees of the US Corporation where they work under contract.*

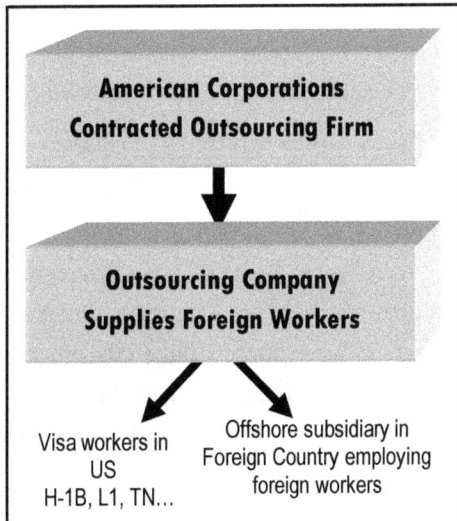

American Corporations Hired Foreign Workers

→ Visa workers in US H-1B, L1, TN...

→ Offshore subsidiary in Foreign Country employing foreign

American Corporations Contracted Outsourcing Firm

↓

Outsourcing Company Supplies Foreign Workers

→ Visa workers in US H-1B, L1, TN...

→ Offshore subsidiary in Foreign Country employing foreign workers

Either way, Americans are displaced by foreign workers.

To clear up another misconception, *outsourcing is not synonymous with sending our jobs overseas*. In the 1990's, *the majority of outsourcing was done inside the United States*. In 2004, over 70% of outsourcing was still being done inside the US. [80] When outsourced work is done in a foreign country, such as China or India, it is offshore outsourcing. It is common for offshore outsourcing to just be called outsourcing, thus the misconception that outsourcing is synonymous with sending work overseas. It is important to understand that the two are linked, because *outsourcing to visa workers in America was the first step towards offshoring our jobs*.

Outsourcing Failed to Deliver Cost Savings

Where was the media coverage to warn American businesses that outsourcing companies often failed to deliver the cost savings promised?

- *46% of the outsourcing contracts never provided any savings a 1998 investigation found.* [523]

- *50% of outsourcing deals failed to deliver the value promised according to a 2003 investigation.*

- *80% of clients experienced problems such as failures to meet time commitments, failures to meet performance requirements, and cost overruns a 2004 study reported.* [80]

- *70% were dissatisfied reported a 2005 survey of 25 major corporations that had outsourced $50 billion in work found that. Almost 50% did not receive promised cost savings.* [80] [122]

As early as 2000, lawsuits from failed outsourcing projects were a growing field for litigation. Outsourcing clients were so dissatisfied that 53% of outsourcing customers renegotiated their contract. In 25% of the renegotiation cases the outsourcing company lost the contract due to customer dissatisfaction. [132]

Outsourcing Customer Support Caused Lost Revenues

US companies grabbed onto customer service outsourcing contracts based on rosy presentations. They weren't warned about thorns such as high customer defection rates that far outweighed the purported savings. [83] A 2006 analysis found an estimated *80% of companies that tried outsourcing customer support did not get the cost savings promised, and 60% lost customers.* [503] For example, Dell computer had to stop sending corporate customer support calls to Bangalore, India due to a flood of complaints. In 2003, *Technology News* reported that *more than half of Dell's 44,300 employees are overseas foreign workers.* [126]

Did Outsourcing Cause US Company Failures?

Outsourcing companies pitched their "services" to CEO's who were not tech savvy, and were easily lured by large bonuses based on *projected cost savings.* [132] After laying off Americans, if executives realized outsourcing was a big mistake, it was too late. They were pawns of the outsourcing company. It was safer to cover-up, than to expose that they got big bonuses for ruining the company, harming shareholders, and for laying off loyal talented American workers.

A Global IT Outsourcing Study found that by 2005 a shocking 49% of outsourcing contracts were terminated early. *The number one reason the outsourcing firms gave for the contract terminations was that their customer went out of business.* [510]

"The New Corporate Reality: External and Market Considerations" a 2005 report warned that *prior to offshoring US companies needed to fully examine the impact to determine whether offshoring will destroy their economic and social base at home.* [615] Offshoring was like persuading someone with a beautiful home on a cliff near the beach to dig away under its foundation to add a slide to get down to the beach faster They foolishly weakened the foundation and soon the whole house was sliding down the cliff. Unfortunately many US companies will not be able to recover.

What Was India Getting?

So why did India continue to aggressively pursue outsourcing? What were they getting out of these failed deals? *While outsourcing often fails to deliver cost savings, it always results in "knowledge transfer" because the outsourcing company's employees gain access to proprietary strategic business and technical data.* [523]

Outsourcing "Hollows Out" American Companies

Walter Shawlee, president of Sphere Research saw through the deceptions in 2005. He said: *"While layoffs seem to make companies look good on the balance sheet and in the stock market, they irretrievably hollow out businesses in terms of real ability and product quality."* Executives were testifying to Congress that we had a high tech worker shortage, while shamefully laying off hundreds of thousands of American high tech workers. Shawlee called this *"the worst kind of duplicity."* [451]

Why Executives Continued to Offshore

Our politicians may be surprised to learn that cheaper foreign workers were not the main reason for offshoring. The main reason US companies went offshore were foreign government enticements in the form of lower taxes and other incentives. [615] Politicians may also be surprised that healthcare costs were a major factor driving American companies to move US jobs overseas. [271]

Outsourcing Mega Deals

The year of our dotcom crash was *also a peak year for outsourcing mega deals.* There were 24 IT mega deals that totaled $54 billion. An April 2010 article, "End of the Era of Mega Outsourcing Deals," reported that 11 of the mega deals signed in 2000 were expiring. [968] Yet in 2011, "508 Outsourcing Deals Signed in Q1 2011: Report," in *The Economic Times* said that outsourcing was growing. BPO deals with Banks, Financial Services, and Insurance made up 34% of the deals. [969] How can banks and financial firms we just bailed out, then turn their backs on Americans who rescued them?

Government Contractors–H-1Bs & Offshore

Contractors were getting rich off our taxes while they displaced Americans with H-1Bs. [205] To name just a few companies getting big federal contracts in 2001:

- *Lockheed ($3 billion), Northrop Grumman ($1 billion), Raytheon ($1 billion), Electronic Data Systems ($970 million), AT&T ($796 million), TRW ($922 million), Boeing ($788 million), Dell ($455 million), Unisys ($452 million), Motorola ($373 million), IBM ($359 million), Verizon ($209 million), WorldCom ($201 million), Oracle ($174 million), Lucent ($157 million), Honeywell ($156 million), KPMG ($150 million), PricewaterhouseCoopers($126 million), Carlyle Group ($112 million) ...[137]*

Now we will answer the question of why many companies were investing overseas operations instead of in the US. A study, "Are You Paying for Corporate Fat Cats?" found 61% of US corporations *"paid no corporate income taxes between 1996 and 2000."* American companies used offshore loopholes to avoid paying taxes, including *"24 of the largest federal contractors."* [689] So these contractors were getting rich off our taxes while transferring our money, technology and jobs to foreign nations!

Executives who took advantage of these tax breaks looked like they were brilliant managers earning fantastic returns. What they were really doing was inflating profits by avoiding paying US taxes. Some companies set up offshore divisions that consisted of a PO Box.

The Institute of Electrical and Electronic Engineering (IEEE) in 2004, *requested that our government stop providing companies financial incentives for offshoring, and begin enforcing intellectual property export controls.* The IEEE emphasized that protecting American jobs and technology was vital to our economy and national security. [88]

To keep from paying US taxes, companies like Intel and HP reinvested their profits in foreign countries. *The big winner profiting from the tax deferment was India.* [134] Consider for example that Hewlett Packard was reported to have kept $14.4 billion of foreign earnings in tax deferment.

Our Government's Secret Role in American Job Losses

One of the biggest secrets is that <u>the largest employer outsourcing our jobs to foreign workers is our own government</u>. *You are good enough to tax, but too expensive to hire!* Our government has been called, *"the biggest shopper on the planet."* For example, in 2001 alone, it bought $235 billion worth of goods and services. [135]

Government spending has been especially lucrative for Information Technology (IT) outsourcing companies. [220] *"U.S. governments are increasingly using India to manage everything from <u>accounting</u> to their food stamp programs. Even the U.S. Postal Service is sending work to India. Automobile engineering and drug research could be next."* [300]

*"<u>The large amount of taxpayer-paid computer work performed by non-citizens for at least 12 state governments and 9 federal agencies is **a scandal crying out for investigation**</u>." Wrote the Phyllis Schlafly Report in a 2003 article, "What the Global Economy Costs Americans:"* [63]

- ■ *Our state and local governments signed $10 billion in technology outsourcing contracts in 2003. These contracts were predicted to more than double reaching $23 billion by 2008.* [140]

- ■ *California outsourced $76.6 million to technical services companies in 2002. State officials signing these contracts did not know how much of this money was going to pay foreign workers.* [105]

- ■ *Taxpayers in New Mexico were outraged in 2003 when they discovered that foreigner programmers worked for their Taxation and Revenue Department, and the state helped them get green cards.*

- ■ *Taxpayers in New Jersey were also outraged when they discovered that the state had hired contractors who then subcontracted welfare service support calls to Bombay, India.* [63]

Often government officials signing these contracts did not know how much of this work is being done by foreign workers in the US, and how much is being sent overseas. By 2005, forty states were offshoring the administration of electronic cards for food stamps. [141]

Chapter 15

Insourcing Myth

It's like having someone take your wallet, and then offer to pay you.

We shouldn't object to outsourcing because we benefit from foreign nations insourcing – right? Well not exactly. A growing US backlash was building in response to Americans' job losses to foreign workers. So, executives and foreign countries used the insourcing myth to diffuse outsourcing protests.

The most frequently used insourcing examples are Japanese automakers that employee Americans who produce cars in America for sale in America. [95] But really this only helped prevent job losses, because Americans were already producing automobiles to sell in the US market. This caused less economic damage than importing foreign cars, because at least many American workers were employed. However, the corporate profits belonged to a foreign company, not a US company. Are any of the Japanese cars produced in America exported to Japan or other nations?

"Outsourcing: How Safe is Your Job," a 2004, *Electronic Design* article, by Ron Schneiderman, the VP of Marketing Intelligence for the research firm iSuppli Corp. claimed that sales to Asia were *"keeping American workers employed in semiconductor manufacturing and design jobs."* [129] They cleverly fail to mention that the reason Asia is a big consumer of semiconductors is because US corporations offshored production of computers and other electronic devices.

Misleading Insourcing Studies

Several studies produced misleading data. For example, insourcing analysts used the Bureau of Economic Analysis (BEA) data that tracks foreign businesses owned by US corporations, and US businesses owned by foreign corporations. BEA data does not track jobs lost due to offshore outsourcing to foreign companies. It only considers "the number of jobs" available in each country. It does not count American job losses to H-1Bs working in our country. [69]

Acquisitions Create Illusion of Insourcing Jobs

Acquisitions of US companies are used to craft the illusion of insourcing job creation. For example, an *economictimes.indiatimes.com* 2004 article claimed that foreign companies created almost 6.4 million jobs in America, and paid US workers $350 billion. It further claimed foreign investment helped lessen the impact of the 2001 US recession. [95] While this sounds good, it is very deceptive.

"The vast majority of jobs at foreign owned firms were not created by foreign investment, but rather are the result of the decision of foreign companies to buy up existing U.S. companies." "Outsourcing" a 2004, *Economic Recovery Review* article by Dean Baker found the claims of foreign investment creating jobs for Americans were false. [68]

Foreign companies were buying American companies. The American employees were then considered "insourced." In reality no jobs were created. In fact, many Americans lost their jobs when buyers brought in foreign visa workers and started offshoring.

From 1998 to 2000, foreign companies spent $900 billion acquiring US companies, while US companies only spent $419 billion buying foreign companies. [488] Even more significant was the big difference in what was being bought. American workers were getting the short end of the stick in both types of deals. *Buying American companies allowed foreign nations to acquire advanced US technology.* [488] US companies in stark contrast often bought foreign companies to acquire cheap foreign workers to cloak US job transfers. [229]

Staff with Foreign Visa Workers

Another insourcing deception relates to the difference in how US offshore and foreign insourcing companies were staffed. For example, a US corporate subsidiary in China would hire mostly Chinese employees. A US corporate subsidiary in India would hire mostly Indian employees. In stark contrast some foreign owned firms operating inside our country hired many H-1B and L-1 visa workers from their country of origin. So, Americans lost jobs when foreign companies insourced, and Americans lost jobs when American companies offshored work to foreign countries.

Illusion of Creating Jobs

Foreign outsourcing companies knew that US corporations were leery of the risks from offshoring. So, they set up outsourcing offices inside the US in the 1990's. Outsourcing then became an easy sell when they showed US executives they could get huge bonuses based on "projected cost savings." *These foreign outsourcing firms cunningly claimed that America is an importer of high tech jobs even though these jobs did not exist in a foreign country.* This was not importing jobs for Americans. Instead it was invading America with foreign workers taking American's jobs. There is a significant difference.

To understand what has been going on, imagine that to get the contract the outsourcing company agrees to hire 900 out of the client's current 1,000 American information technology (IT) workers. At this point the outsourcing company may claim it created 900 American jobs when in fact it cut 100 jobs. Next, they import 200 low paid H-1Bs that the Americans are required to train. As the H-1Bs are trained, they layoff more Americans and import more H-1Bs. And, so the pattern goes. Despite causing hundreds of Americans to lose their jobs, the outsourcing company claims to be creating American jobs. Compounding the damage, they used these H-1B visa workers in the US to communicate with offshore workers laying the groundwork for later offshoring the jobs.

Only a Few Americans Benefited

With regard to insourcing generating income for Americans, foreign outsourcing companies did pay a lot for: American PR companies to develop propaganda, persuading our politicians to pass H-1B and other harmful legislation, American law firms to assistance with immigration and contracts, US media to promote outsourcing, and to get US accounting firms to claim cost savings from outsourcing. So, a few Americans did make a lot of money–but they made the money at the expense of millions of Americans harmed.

In a turn of poetic justice, the Americans who got rich 'transferring' our jobs to foreign workers, will not be needed anymore after our jobs are offshored, so they too will lose their income, home, insurance, and more.

It is Time to Tell Americans the Truth

The net impact of "insourcing" from foreign acquisitions and foreign outsourcing contracts to America is highly destructive.

Our government allowed foreign owned outsourcing businesses to staff up their US offices hiring foreign visa workers. [516] This violated the premise that the H-1B was approved to help American companies be globally competitive.

Our own government promoted the insourcing myth. For example, in 2004, the US Labor Secretary Elaine L. Chao said that the number of US jobs lost to foreign countries *"was far outweighed by the number of jobs in the United States at foreign owned companies."* [68] If outsourcing, insourcing, and offshoring were in fact benefiting America it would be reflected in our trade deficit. In 2004, when she made this claim the US trade deficit was already almost $600 billion annually. [68]

Chapter 16

India Dominates Outsourcing &

Offshoring

Following the trail of our professional job losses

W hile India took about 50% of H-1B visas per year, its domination of US high tech jobs that were offshored was even greater. For example, in 2002, India took 85% of our software jobs that were offshored. [774]

"US Gives India Assurance on Outsourcing," a 2003 *Times of India* article by Chidanand Rajghatta reported the Bush Administration reassured India that our government would make no effort to stem the offshoring of our jobs.

India was on track to reach its goal of $20 billion in outsourcing revenues by 2008. Most of this outsourcing money would come out of our country. [86]

How did India pull this off?

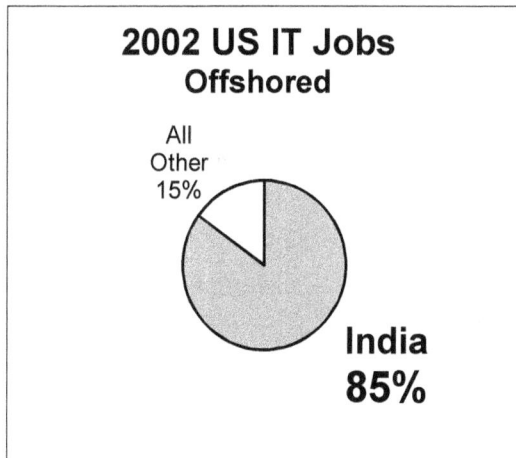

2002 US IT Jobs Offshored

All Other 15%

India 85%

Indian Immigrant US Corporate "Body Shops"

Syntel, Mastech, and Cognizant are *"minority" US companies founded by immigrants from India*.

In 1992 Syntel became *one of the first US companies to provide onsite project management consultations for American corporations, and then offshore the software development to India*. In 1998, *Syntel* with revenues of $160 million, *admitted in 1998 that **H-1Bs made up 66% of its US workforce*.** [468] Syntel was, founded in 1980 by Bharat Desai and Neerja Sethi. Its business partners included: IBM, Sun Microsystems, TIBCO, Oracle, and others. [724] A 2000 *Baltimore Sun* article, "Indentured Servants for High-Tech Trade Labor," claimed Syntel supplied contract workers to *Ford, Kmart, DaimlerChrysler, an insurance company, and a state government*. [468]

Mastech founded by Sunil Wadhwai and Ashok Trivedi *has employees in five cities in India: Bangalore, Chennai, Noida, and Pune*. Tripti Noorani VP of Immigration and Compliance helped get ***20,000 H-1B Visas and 2,000 Green Cards*** *for Mastech employees*. [725] The *Baltimore Sun* article reported that Mastech executives *contributed to Senator Spencer Abraham's campaign around the time he sponsored the 1998 H-1B quota increase*. Mastech had revenues of almost $400 million and *admitted that **H-1Bs made up nearly 35%** of its US workers*. The article reported that GE *planned to acquire a $30 million share in Mastech*; and then over a *three year period to purchase $122 million in outsourcing services* from Mastech. [468] Mastech *even had a contract to work on White House computers.* [468]

Cognizant Technology Solutions based in New Jersey, paid its CEO Kumar Mahadeva $27 million in 2003. This made Mahadeva one of the highest paid executives in the world. **Cognizant *employed 70% of its workforce in India*** —almost 12,000 workers. Moreover, Cognizant planned to open a software development center in China. [6]

India's Outsourcing Firms in America

India's outsourcing companies did tedious Y2K work to gain access to our IT services industry. [300] Once established in the US they then targeted our IT services—a $240 billion a year industry. Following our dotcom crash their revenues soared.

"Indentured Servants for High-Tech Trade Labor," a 2000 *Baltimore Sun* article exposed how H-1B visas were abused. [468] [96] Body shops *"take advantage of the well-meaning visa applicants as the latter, mostly unqualified, are funneled into the US by middlemen who help them with fake academic degrees and pad their resumes in order to secure the H-1B visas"* [32] Were H-1Bs innocent victims if they knowingly took Americans' jobs using fake credentials?

By exploiting H-1B and L1 visas body shops could under bid contractors employing Americans. Outsourcers got rich. [33] They *billed as much as four times what they were paying the visa workers.* [338]

"The Infosys Financial Model" *expected to pay about $6,000 per American displaced. The model notes that it is much more expensive in Germany where the cost is 100,000 Deutsch Marks.* [540] Infosys's quarterly net profit for the fourth quarter in 2006 jumped 52.4% to $218 million. The company added 43 new clients including *Goldman Sachs, and J. C. Penny. Infosys was negotiating several huge outsourcing deals, but refused to disclose the company names.*

Wipro sales jumped 43% in 2004. Wipro claimed to be the *"world's largest third-party R&D provider."* It was selling infrastructure management, financial services and product testing. [597] A 2005, *US News and World Report* article, "Bangalore's Big Dreams," reported Azim Premji, a Muslim who owns 84% of Wipro, became the *"richest man in India."* He got a BS degree from Stanford University. [122]

Critics claimed foreign owned outsourcing companies were breaking US laws by their hiring practices. For example, in 2004, *zazona.com* reported that Tata favored hiring young upper caste males from India to work in the US. [153]

Business Process Outsourcing (BPO)

"Indian BPO Guy: Hero or Villain?" a 2004 article told how immigrants from India were making a fortune persuading US companies to *offshore "accounting, auditing, telemarketing, research, tax preparation, and technical writing jobs."* They called it *"efficient employment"* when they displaced an American with a worker in India for *"one third the cost."* They complained that the *"world harps on globalization and free trade policies,"* while they, *"modestly"* help millions in *their native country get jobs and dream big.* [98] (*Sounds like Charles Dicken's Uriah Heep.*)

Atul Vashistha defended outsourcing saying, *"I feel that somebody has to speak up for it, and you know I have made a career out of globalization."* [379] He came to the US on a student visa in 1989 to pursue an MBA. He was granted citizenship. In 1999, he founded neoIT. By 2003 neoIT had a billion dollars in BPO contracts. About 70% of this money along with 50,000 US jobs went to India. Imagine one immigrant from India causing 50,000 Americans to lose jobs they needed to support their families. [379] And, Vashistha is not the only one, the article said scores are *"emerging from the shadows."* [98]

A July 2003, *EETimes* article, "India's Tech Industry Defends H-1B, Outsource Roles" by K.C. Krishnadas, reported India had 170 IT companies with 60,000 employees in the US. India was worried we may cut back on the H-1B visas i.e. *"India's software exports industry."* So, it claimed offshoring $142 billion in services to India by 2009, would create a *net savings for the US economy of $390 billion, because it would cost $532 billion if the work was done in the US.* [123] The Economic Circulation Model shown earlier disproves these cost savings claims.

Indian CEO's Meet Team Obama

"H-1B: Indian CEOs Meet Obama Team" a 2009 article reported *business executives from India had already met with the Obama team, and were reassured the H-1B program would continue as would offshoring of American jobs to India.* [735] This violated Obama's campaign promises to Americans.

Who Employs the Most Visa Workers?

How can a visa program approved to help protect our nation's technology leadership be used by companies challenging our technology leadership?

- *In 2002 Indian owned outsourcing companies in the list of companies employing the most H-1Bs included: Mastech, Tata Consultancy, Syntel, Wipro, Tata Infotech/Tata Unisys, HCL America ...[338]*

- *In 2006, the top ten companies that hired H-1Bs were: Infosys (India), Wipro (India), Microsoft (USA), Tata (India), Satyam (India), Cognizant Technology Solutions (India), Patni Computer Systems (India), IBM (USA), Oracle (USA), and Larsen & Toubro Infotech (India). Moreover, from 2007 to 2012 Infosy planned to hire 29,448 H-1Bs, and Wipro planned to hire 24,012 H-1Bs.[665]*

In 2003, 50% of Tata's 5,000 US workers were L-1s, 33% of Infosys's 3,000 US workers were L-1s, and 32% of Wipro's US workers were L-1s. [63]

H-1B Contract Lawsuit

Body shops got visas approved and paid INS and legal fees. [31] In return H-1Bs' are required to sign restrictive contracts. [479]

An H-1B from India sued a body shop that demanded a $77,085 finder's fee when he accepted a job with its US client. The H-1B was awarded $215,050. [56] Ironically, H-1Bs were hired because they could be exploited.

Young American college graduates denied job opportunities, and Americans who lost their jobs because of visa fraud are the ones most deserving of a legal remedy.

Chapter 17

Dotcom Attack on US Stock Market

"Bad gains are truly losses."–*Ben Franklin*

While the dotcom crash happened in April 2000, once you begin digging you discover it set the stage for *our current economic crisis*. This is the starting point that launched the offshoring boom that created our "decade of job losses" that Tankersly wrote about. And our banks and venture capital followed to fund the offshore boom.

During the dotcom boom our media was saturated with buzzwords like *"New Economy"* aka *"New Paradigm"* to persuade Americans earnings were irrelevant when picking stocks. If it was a dotcom company, it was supposed to be a good investment. However, most of the dotcoms in reality had no solid business foundation. It was deceptive nonsense that were it not for the magnitude of harm, it would be almost funny how people were misled by the pied piper media playing the buzzwords. [294] [295] [296]

Why did our media hype dotcom stocks? Major US news networks including *ABC, NBC, and CBS* received a lot of revenue from dotcom advertising. These networks rode the dotcom wave. The more US citizens invested in dotcom stock, the more money they received in advertising. There appears to be a conflict of interest with the media reporting news on its advertising sponsors. [299]

False Prophets of False Profits

Accounting deceptions proliferated that artificially inflated dotcom earnings. An article, "The Nasdaq Bubble," observed: *"The New Economy was a farce, and traditional economic principles still hold."* [294]

During the dotcom boom, our Big 5 accounting firms included: *Arthur Andersen, Price Waterhouse Coopers, Deloitte & Touche, Ernst & Young, and KPMG. Unbeknownst to most Americans our Big 5 accounting firms were employing foreign H-1Bs and offshore foreign workers.* [387] These were the firms selling consulting services and creating financial documents claiming big cost savings for displacing Americans with foreign workers. Therefore, *a conflict of interest not only existed at the management level it permeated down to the accountants and consultants.* [778]

H-1Bs may be responsible for massive dotcom accounting fraud. In 2000, at the peak of the dotcom boom, the top 20 employers of H-1Bs included our big accounting firms:

■ *Mastech Corp, Tata Consultancy Computer People, Oracle, PricewaterhouseCoopers LLP, Lucent, Motorola, Syntel, Intelligroup, Comsys Technical, Deloitte & Touche LLP, KPMG Peat Marwick LLP, Cisco, Keane, Ernst & Young LLP, Intel, SAI Software Consultants, Indotronix, Complete Business Solutions, Computer Horizons Corp.* [400]

When Arthur Andersen was felled by the Enron scandal *only 28,000 of its 85,000 employees worked in the US. And, it employed H-1Bs, so many of its US workers were not Americans.* ***Most of its workers were foreign****.*

Former SEC Chairman Arthur Levitt woefully observed: *"Managing may be giving way to manipulation. Integrity may be losing out to illusion."* [296] Renowned economist John Kenneth Galbraith said: *"I've been looking at auditors' signatures all my life, but I will never again do so without some doubts as to their validity. There must be the strongest public and legal pressure to get honest competent accounting."* [1]

Many dotcom insiders cashed in with some taking returns in the *"**thousands of percent**."* [296] While dotcoms were hyped as *"New Economy"* companies, they were using old accounting tricks.

RECORDING REVENUES THAT WEREN'T THERE

One trick was recording revenues before they happened. In 1999, new SEC guidelines targeted dotcoms suspected of not accurately reporting revenues. Over 30 dotcom companies had to restate their earnings. Many no longer looked like stellar performers. [296]

BARTERING ADS TO DECEIVE INVESTORS

One slick accounting trick involved *bartering of advertising.* Dotcom companies would display banner ads on each others' websites, and then *each company would record a million in revenues from advertising and a million in expenses. In reality, no revenues were generated.* It was a deceptive scheme to create counterfeit dotcom revenues. [296]

PUMP AND DUMP

Swindlers buy stock and pump up the price with media hype and then dump (i.e. sell) the stock. During the dotcom boom, online bulletin board tipsters *claimed to be objective; however, many may have been company insiders, large stockholders or even paid fraudsters.* [292]

SHADY REVERSING INFLATE FINANCIAL STATEMENTS

Another trick was "reversing"—i.e. claiming pure profits on inventory that had been written down to zero. Because of accounting rules it was hard to pin down as a crime. However, *reverses not properly disclosed misled investors when the reverses significantly inflated income.* [344]

PONZI SCHEME (PYRAMID)

An article, "Up, Up and Away: CEO Compensation" in 2000, likened the dotcom to a Ponzi (pyramid) scheme. CEOs quietly cashed out while using the media to hype the stocks. [2]

INFLATING OFFSHORE "PROFITS"

US companies charged overseas costs against US operations. This falsely understated US earnings so they could cut or eliminate taxes paid to our government and justify laying off Americans. *This deceptive accounting practice made offshore operations look much more attractive to investors than they actually were.* [33]

IT Analysts Conflicts of Interest During Dotcom Era

Our media relied on IT analysts for recommendations on dotcom and technology companies. *While financial analysts are required to disclose if they were helping to market a product, IT analysts were not required to disclose such conflicts of interest.* "Scrutinizing the Scrutineers: How Accurate are High Technology's Pithy Pundits?" a 1998 story wrote: *"It's a tricky business, with technology firms, public relations organizations, computer analysts and the media all tangled in the same web. However, no one in the industry appears to doubt the impact analysts have on either the companies for which they work or the public that buys the product they comment on."* [365]

Stock Market Scam Theory

Most dotcoms were run by inept entrepreneurs who *did not have business plans or earnings to merit the soaring valuations of their stocks.* [294] [295]

Dotcom Startups		
Stock Market Scam Theory		
Scam Phases	**Inside Investors**	**US Citizen Investors**
Phase I: Startup	Insiders pay $1 per share for 5 million shares = **Invested $5 million**	
Phase II: Use media hype, accounting tricks and bribes to drive up stock price.	Stock skyrockets = Founders became multimillionaires based on stock valuations. So they claim to be "genius" entrepreneurs.	Americans hear about skyrocketing stocks and "genius" entrepreneurs and IPO.
Phase III: Insiders take company public and sell overvalued stock at peak.	Stocks peak at $100 per share. Insiders do a "planned" sell of 2 million shares = **Take $200 million**. Still own 3 Million shares	The American public buys 2 million shares at peak for $100 per share = **Invested $200 million**.
Phase IV: Market correction. Stock plummets.	Stock plummets to $1 per share. Scammers still hold 3 million shares at $1 = $3 Million.	Stock **plummets to $1** per share. Americans lose $197 Million

The genius lies in that Scammers still own stock as "cover" when they took $200 million on their investment of $5 million.

Dotcom Not a Normal Bubble

The US stock market dotcom wild climb and devastating fall did not fit normal patterns. The NASDAQ exploded from 600 companies in 1996 to 5,000 companies in 2000. [294]

Then the dotcom crash hit in April 2000. [294] The _NASDAQ dropped by $3.33 trillion_—one analyst estimated this was the value of over 1/3 of the houses in the US. [355]

The dotcom boom was fueled by media claims about the "_New Economy._" It all sounds impressive until you discover that it was not true.

In his 2002 book, _Conquer the Crash_, Robert R. Prechter Jr. revealed that the US has not experienced anything even close to a "_New Economy._" He compared the US economic expansion of 1974–2000 (dotcom), to the US economic expansion of 1942–1966.

He found _the dotcom economic expansion was weaker: The Gross Domestic Product average annual real growth rate was weaker, the industrial production average annual gain was weaker, the capacity utilization was lower, and the monthly average unemployment rate was worse._ Logically you then would expect the Dow Jones Industrial Average (DJIA) gain to be less during the dotcom 1974 – 2000 expansion. Instead he discovered that _the DJIA gain during this time period was double the amount of for the stronger bull market period from 1942–1966._ (p. 6–9)

Even more surprising his "Year-End Stock Market Valuation" graphic shows the normal range for the stock price to book value ratio runs between 1 to 2. The 1990's dotcom stock market skewed severely off this normal pattern. His chart shows the most extreme stock overvaluation peak occurred in 2000 with the ratio at an astounding 10. [21] This means that when _millions of Americans lost money in the dotcom crash, stocks overvaluations were running 5 to 10 times the book value._ [21]

Foreign Investment Drove Dotcom Boom

Silicon Valley was the epicenter of the dotcom boom. [305] *"Foreign investment was a major contributor to the U.S. stock bubble."* [362] From 1990–2000 foreigners "invested" 6 trillion dollars in the US, while Americans only invested about 2.5 trillion in other countries. [355] Total venture capital investments, foreign and domestic, in the US soared from about $15 billion in 1996, to *almost $120 billion dollars in 2000.* [462] This massive flow of capital appears to have primed the pump for the largest stock market dump in history.

In mid 2001, a Canadian consultant called the dotcom debacle *"venture capital disease."* He said Canada was not "infected" and the dotcom crash was primarily an American phenomenon. [296]

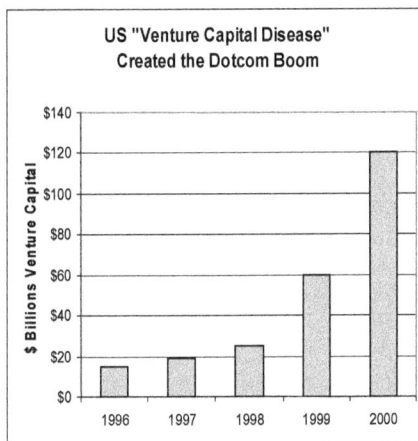

US "Venture Capital Disease" Created the Dotcom Boom

"Dotcom Titians" Blocked Law Protecting Investors

"Dotcom titans" were worried about being sued 3 years before the crash. *In 1997, a network of Silicon Valley CEOs, including "dotcom titans," banned together in opposition to a California initiative that would have made it easier for shareholders to sue companies that mismanaged their investments. They formed TechNet in 1997, led by* John Doerr *co-founder of the Silicon Valley venture capital firm Kleiner Perkins Caufield & Byers (KPCB) who "had a stake in more than 250 technology ventures."* Doerr *"helped raise a record $40 million to oppose the shareholder proposition, ensuring its defeat."* [559]

One of TechNet's "Accomplishments" from *"giving senior executives a voice in national politics,"* was that it: *"Maintained favorable accounting treatment for stock options granted to outside directors by defeating the Financial Standards Accounting Board's proposal that these options be expensed."* [558]

Immigrant Entrepreneurial Genius?

In the 1990's, much of the foreign investment in the US came from Asian sources, and *the money was almost exclusively available to Asian born entrepreneurs*. The foreign *venture capital that flowed into the US was actually much greater than the numbers reported because foreign investment by individuals living in Asia also radically increased during our dotcom boom*. [372].

AnnaLee Saxenian's "Silicon Valley's New Immigrant Entrepreneurs," 2000 study found that Chinese and Indian networks were *prolific in raising venture capital for entrepreneurs from their ethnic group*. She found *almost no membership overlap, and that each* network provided mentoring to "*co-ethnic entrepreneurs*." For example, Alpine Technology Ventures funded Chinese immigrants' startups. The Draper International Fund financed startups formed by immigrants from India. InveStar Capital helped fund entrepreneurs from Taiwan. [372]

Dun and Bradstreet studied 11,443 high tech startups in Silicon Valley from 1980 to 1996 and found that 17% of the CEOs had Chinese surnames, and 7% had Indian surnames. However, Saxenian said this method "*may understate the scale of immigrant entrepreneurship because firms that were started by Chinese or Indians but have hired non-Asian outsiders as CEO's are not counted*." [372]

Immigrant founded startups could outspend other startups. [294] The money and cheap labor created the illusion that they were entrepreneurial geniuses. On top of that they got minority benefits. But their biggest advantage was network collaboration. They would *link startups to network contacts working in US corporations, and network contacts working in US federal, state, and local governments*. They would "*make use of the technology being developed by a friend of theirs*." [128]

The Asian American Manufacturing Association (AAMA) helped launch Chinese startups in America. The AAMA linked engineers with investment bankers, consultants in advisory roles to American business leaders, lawyers for leveraging the US legal system to their advantage, and *accountants dedicated to making offshoring to the Pacific Rim look financially appealing*. [372]

Synchronized Attack on US Stock Market

The synchronization of foreign born executives entering the upper echelons of major high tech US corporations, paralleled by the foreign born entrepreneurs starting dotcom companies was too coordinated to be just a coincidence. They were interrelated. The unprecedented number of dotcom startups manipulated the demand for internet computer servers and caused stock prices to soar for companies like Cisco, Sun Microsystems, and Intel. [299]

During the boom from 1995–1999, our stock market experienced bizarre growth rates. The NASDAQ jumped over 40% per year. This crazy climb peaked in March 2000. Then the dotcom bust took the US stock market on a terrible dive. The "New Economy" telecom infrastructure companies soon followed in 2001. *Cisco dropped 78%. Nortel dropped 90%, and JDS Uniphase dropped 91%.* [364]

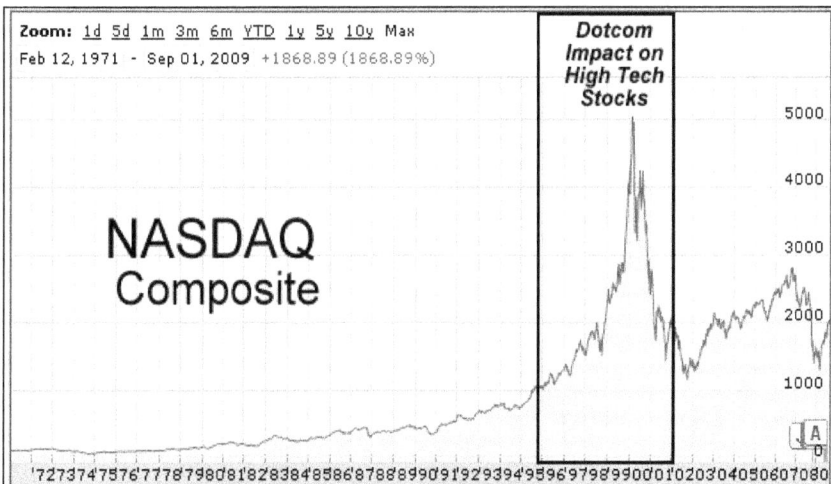

And it is not just China and India, the Organization of Pakistani Entrepreneurs of North America (OPEN) saw Silicon Valley as the place to launch global businesses run by Pakistani-Americans. They also targeted our high tech companies, research universities, and venture capital firms. [644] How many more ethnic networks are there?

Forbes List Out-of-Whack

"<u>Never have so many companies worth so much had so little revenue,</u>" wrote *Forbes* in March 2000. Its *Forbes 500* list of top companies included 892 companies–*the largest in its 32 year history.* [367] Most of the new companies on the list were dotcom or dotcom related. To make the list based on sales a company must have revenues of at least $2.6 billion. However, 172 of the companies made less than $250 million. Instead, *market capitalization got them on the list.* [367]

- *Market capitalization is the number of outstanding shares times the current market price per share. For example, if a company has 1 million shares outstanding and the current price per share is $100 then the market capitalization of the company is $100 million.*

Just weeks after the report the dotcoms began to fall like flies. Market values plummeted. *Almost 50 of the new companies would not have been included in the Forbes 500 list had the data been gathered four weeks later.* Many of these companies were teetering on going out of business. [367]

Two years later, *Fortune* published, "The Greedy Bunch" Qwest *Communications was at the top of the list*: a Director, sold $1.57 billion, and a former CEO sold $230 million. [369]

- *"Qwest Lawsuits Settled" a 2004 Denver Business Journal article, reported shareholders sued directors and officers for "breach of fiduciary duty." Attorneys told shareholders that this Denver based company was incorporated in Delaware, and advised that <u>Delaware law would make it difficult to win an insider trading case against the company officers and directors.</u> [373] How many dotcoms were incorporated in Delaware?*

- *Two years later, a 2006, Salt Lake City Desert News article, "Settlement is Approved in Qwest Lawsuit," said a $400 million settlement was reached on a consolidated lawsuit that "accused Qwest Communications of civil fraud in connection with a multibillion-dollar <u>accounting scandal.</u>" Qwest agreed to compensate shareholders. The settlement covered Qwest and several executives with the exception of a former CEO and a former CFO. [756]*

SEC "Protecting Big Financial Predators"?

Our Securities and Exchange Commission (SEC) failed to protect Americans from dotcom fraud.

After the crash, Bush made Harvey Pitt Chairman of the SEC. "SEC Needs New Leader," a 2002 article by Jack Anderson and Douglas Cohn said that Pitt *"fought proposals from his predecessor, Arthur Leavitt to end the practice whereby accounting firms could act both as auditors and consultants to the same corporation. This obvious conflict of interest for accounting firms is at the root of the current accounting scandals."* They said this practice *should have never been allowed in the first place.* They noted that Pitt had been *"legal counsel for Arthur Andersen, LLP, the auditor and consultant of beleaguered Enron."* [778]

Pitt hired McKinsey to help uncover fraud in big business—even though McKinsey sold consulting services to big business. Critics objected because Enron's Jeff Skilling had previously been a high level executive at McKinsey.

"S.E.C.'s Embattled Chief Resigns in Wake of Latest Political Storm," the *New York Times* reported in 2002 that the Bush White House *"welcomed" Harvey Pitt's resignation.* [755]

Pitt was gone, but shockingly McKinsey was allowed to continue an *inside analysis of the SEC.* A 270 page non-public 2003 report *"prepared by SEC staffers and McKinsey consultants"* claimed the SEC was short on resources. It found that only *one third of SEC investigations were done internally.* And, almost *half of the internal investigations consisted of reading newspapers.* [388] Were two thirds outsourced!?

■   *In a Fox News story, "Madoff Tipster Blasts SEC, Says He Feared for His Safety." Harry Markopolos told a House hearing that he had warned the SEC for a decade about Bernard Madoff's operations. Investors lost $50 billion. Markopolos testified, "the SEC is busy protecting the big financial predators from investors." He said, "I became fearful for the safety of my family," and that Madoff had so much power he was "in a position to end careers or worse."* [719] *Why didn't the SEC heed his warnings?*

Where did the Dotcom Money Go?

Dotcom companies, as other software companies, had very low startup and overhead expense. Unlike manufacturing companies that can lose millions in manufacturing facilities and high cost parts inventory; software does not require expensive manufacturing facilities and requires minimal inventory costs. So how did US investors lose trillions in the dotcom bust? It cannot be explained in inventory or in production facilities losses.

Where did the money go? A large portion of the money went into the pockets of the founders of dotcom companies, their network of contacts, and into venture capital companies. This was a tectonic shift in wealth from Americans who worked and earned the money to people who scammed our stock market.

Stock Market Reform

Our economy is dependent on trust in our stock market and financial institutions. Justice for dotcom scam victims is too long delayed. Hardworking Americans were scammed by dotcom companies, financial institutions, and more. There need to be broad scale investigations of people and entities who extracted more than $100,000 from the US stock market from 1980 to present to determine if they unjustly enriched themselves through accounting deceptions or insider trading.

Money and property recovered from insiders found guilty of scams should go into an economic recovery fund to finance American startup businesses that employ American workers. And, it could help American families unjustly financially harmed. For example, it could cover college costs for their children.

Chapter 18

Indian "Mafia's" Dotcom Role

They arrived "nearly broke" as students, and we were taxed to educate them.

They got rich selling dotcom startups, outsourcing, and offshoring.

A January 24, 2000 article, "The Curry Network," posted on *tiecarolinas.org* stated, *"TiE represents only a fraction of what some Silicon Valley executives call the Indian Mafia, a gang that voraciously seeks IPO opportunities. A veritable international hydra, the group's tentacles reach from California to Boston to Bombay to London, always in search of new ideas and serendipitous connections."* [312]

As a group, none compares to the "Indian Mafia" operating in the US during the dotcom boom. In 1998, a report estimated 40% of Silicon Valley startups were *"Indian-spawned."* How much wealth this network created is questionable. However, how much it was able to extract from US corporations and our stock market is astounding.

As shown earlier *India dominated IT outsourcing.* This outsourcing played a major role during the dotcom boom. It is important to note that *"India had barely 6,800" software professionals* in 1985. [335] Yet, twelve short years later in 1997, India was *"quietly but quickly emerging as a leader in the field of software engineering and web-based services."* This would have been impossible if our universities had not been used to educate our competition, and to persuade US software companies that they must outsource to *"retain competitive advantage."* [335]

Over 100,000 Indians Became Millionaires!

At the peak of the dotcom boom more than 100,000 immigrants from India had become millionaires. [192] [350] [359] [310] That year several were listed in the "Forbes Richest 400 Americans" as starting companies claimed to be worth over a billion dollars. *The list included:*

- *Sanjiv Sidhu's startup i2 Technologies (ITWO)*
- *Tibco Software (TIBX)*
- *Gururaj Desh Deshpande's startup Sycamore Networks (SCMR)*
- *Pradeep Sidhu Juniper Networks (JNPR)*
- *Naveen Jain's startup InfoSpace (INSP)*
- *Rajendra Singh (Teligent),*
- *Romesh Wadhwani's startup Aspect Development (bought by i2)* [309]

Using Google Finance to compare stock histories for five of these startups shows a pattern similar to a pump and dump scheme. *Given that Google was in a list of top 100 employers of H-1Bs, the fair use legal protection is invoked for the vital public interest. Also, Google states that it is not liable for any errors or omissions. Therefore, the data must be verified.*

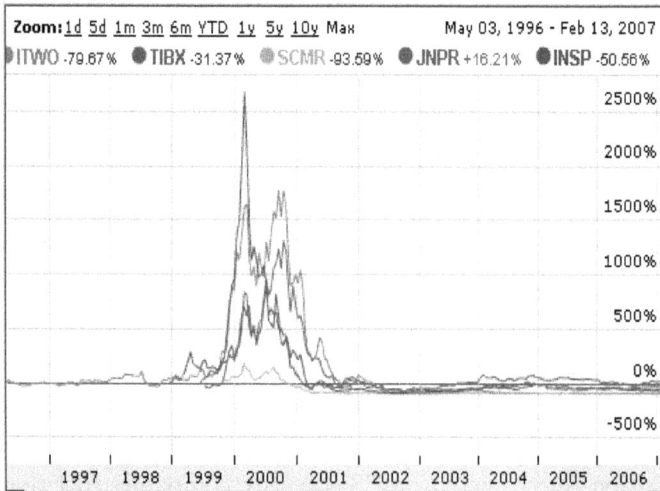

In 2001 Forbes published a new list—a list of dropoffs who are billionaires no more. *Included in this list were: Gururaj E. Deshpande, Naveen Jain, Pradeep Sindhu, Rajendra Singh, Romesh T. Wadhwani.* [371] [395]

Indian "Mafia" Network Takes Root in USA

The seeds for the Indian "Mafia" in the US were planted after WWII when US Aid helped fund and build the Indian Institute of Technology (IIT).

In the 1970's graduates of IIT entered US university graduate schools. They arrived in the United States "nearly broke" [312] which means that we picked up the tab for their education.

Their temporary student visas legally required them to return to India after completing their studies. But, they stayed in our country seeking jobs in the heart of our high tech research and development region—Silicon Valley. They got jobs in US corporations such as Cisco, Intel, and HP. [463] [312]

In 1987, Prakash Chandra founded the Silicon Valley Indian Professionals Association (SIPA). In the early 1990's, *delegates from the government of India traveled to our country, and persuaded SIPA to promote US business relations with India, and to "fill the information gap" for India*. [372] Passage of the 1990 H-1B visa program legislation positioned India to gain insider access to "*fill the information gap*." H-1Bs gained access to closely guarded US technology secrets.

SIPA provided strategic information of interest to, and worked closely with the government of India and Indian businesses. In 1992 Chandra returned to India, and the mantle for India was picked up by The IndUS Entrepreneurs (TiE) organization. [372]

Multiple sources tell the story of how the Indian "Mafia" took root in America. For example, a 2000, article, "The TiE that Binds," tells the progression. First, *they got a degree at IIT or some other technical school in India*. Second, *they obtained a student visa to attend graduate school in the United States*. Third, *they got jobs in Corporate America*. Fourth, *they founded startups that, with the help of the "Mafia" network, they sold to American corporations and/or sold stock in the US stock market to become multimillionaires*. [463]

The IndUS Entrepreneurs (TiE) aka the Indian "Mafia"

TiE was spawned in 1992, when India's Secretary of Electronics traveled to Silicon Valley, USA to meet with Kanwal Rekhi, Suhas Patil, and Prabhu Goel. While waiting on the Minister to arrive, they decided to form the TiE network. [372]

Although TiE claims to not engage in political activities, it traces its origins back to a meeting with a government official from India. And, TiE acknowledges that the Indian Government sought its help. [653] TiE also has connections to our government officials that most Americans do not know about. For example, a 2000 article, "TiE has Helped Create Businesses Worth More Than 200 Billion," claimed that: "*A 200 person TiE delegation was invited to accompany President Bill Clinton to India to meet with the Indian PM earlier this year.*" [653] This was the year of the dotcom crash.

When TiE started in Silicon Valley, its members were 80% first generation immigrants, and 20% second generation immigrants. TiE spread to "*Boston, New York, Dallas, Atlanta, Chicago, Los Angeles, and Washington, D.C.*" as well as to London and multiple cities in India. [653] *Duke professor Vivek Wadhwa mentioned earlier co-founded TiE Carolinas.* [685]

TiE claims to be open and inclusive, yet TiE began as an *exclusive invitation only organization* comprised primarily of immigrants from India and Pakistan. [345] TiE is a tight knit group. Many live in neighborhood clusters in multi-million dollar houses. [331] In 2007, TiE said it was not based on race. That contradicted the "TiE Rockies Speakers 2000-2001" agenda which claimed, "*TiE, a network organization based in Silicon Valley that promotes entrepreneurship among the Indus people.*" [310] i.e. People originating from South Asia. [289]

According to the TiE website *it is the place to come for contacts if looking for money, or advice.* TiE is a network of entrepreneurs, professionals, and *executives in US corporations.* TiE's members sought strategic positions in US Universities, and US industries–*software, IT, biotechnology, services* including *legal, financial*, and more. [592] Recall the "*management thinker*" Mohanbir Sawhney–he was a member of TiE.

Kanwal Rekhi—"Godfather of Indian Dotcommers"

Kanwal Rekhi launched TiE in 1992, because he was angry: "*The genesis of TiE was based in fundamental anger...*" [332] Rekhi was upset when he did not get a promotion and *claimed* a white guy who was "*only half as good as me*" got promoted. His goal was to help "our people" become entrepreneurs. [467] In 1995, Rekhi quit his CTO job at Novell, and focused on TiE where he "*cultivated his Godfather image.*" [463]

Who is Rekhi? He is a Sikh from Kanpur India. He entered the US in 1971 on a *student visa* to pursue a Masters degree at Michigan Tech University. A graduate of IIT Bombay, he arrived with only $10, and lived at the YMCA for $4 per night. Rekhi married an American, and worked in the US as an engineer. [350] [351] [289]

Rekhi and two Indian partners founded Excelan, a computer networking company. Rekhi was CEO. In 1987, they asked a venture capital firm to help them launch an IPO. Rekhi objected when the venture firm wanted to name a former HP executive CEO. However, he agreed after they warned him Americans may not buy the stock. Excelan became *the first Indian startup to receive venture capital funding*. [350] [351] [289] Later Rekhi reclaimed his CEO title. In 1989, Novell bought Excelan for *$210 million*. Rekhi's share made him a millionaire. *Thus began the pattern of the Indian "Mafia" spawned startups, often with token CEO "whiteys," to launch IPOs and/or to sell these startups to major American corporations in multimillion dollar deals.*

"*Upstarts: how India's dotcom pioneers staked their claim in Silicon Valley your space,*" a 2001 article by Ajay Singh in *Asiaweek.com* dubbed Rekhi the "*godfather of Indian dotcommers.*" [359] While most members of the "Mafia" kept a low profile, Rekhi sought publicity. [289]

In December 2000, following our horrific dotcom crash, Rekhi was quoted in the *Hindustan Times*: "*The whole dotcom world was not a robust set-up ... I said in January, that 99 per cent of the companies would fail. There is no value here.*" [358] How many dotcoms did TiE help launch?

TiE = "Deals, Deals, Deals"

"The 'Indian Mafia' Muscles onto the Web," a 1999, *redherring.com* article reported that *many of the startups founded by immigrants from India received their funding with the assistance of TiE.* Reki, referred to as "a Pakistani," and the ""*Godfather" of TiE*," said *Indians seeking venture capital get preferential treatment, "<u>even over whites</u>."* [333] Racism?

At the peak of the dotcom an article in *Fortune*, "The Indians of Silicon Valley," wrote: "*The hidden geniuses of the tech revolution are Indian engineers—here's how one bucked stereotypes, got rich, and has become <u>the godfather to a generation of immigrant entrepreneurs</u>.*" It reported that <u>all the startups Rekhi funded were founded by people from India, and that he made about $500 million</u>. Yet, few people from India were CEO's. Why? *Many became rich not from running their startups, but by <u>selling their startups to large American corporations</u>.* Rekhi's biggest payoff came from helping K.B. Chandrasklar launch Exodus. Rekhi *put in $1 million for a 2% stake estimated to be worth $130 million.* [289]

TiE is called a non-profit yet: "*Every other month, The Indus Entrepreneurs holds its meeting ... The main course is deals, deals, deals. The organization has emerged as a premier deal generator in Silicon Valley.*" [312] An article in 2000, "TiE has helped Create Businesses worth more than $200 Billion," reported that: "*Since its inception TiE has managed to IPO over 50 start-ups—<u>making it more prolific than many venture capital funds</u>.*" [653]

Goldman Sachs and Kleiner Perkins Caufield & Byers and other "big name sponsors" funded TiE's annual conference. [312] *In 1999 TiE claimed that "<u>the leaders of TiE had become multimillionaires</u>."* [467]

"*Isn't there something sinister about what could be perceived as a cliquish nationalist approach?*" David Mildenberg asked Rekhi about his investments in a 2000 article "Networking Godfather to Visit Triangle." Rekhi responded that TiE had members from both India and Pakistan. [351]

By 2001, Rekhi helped fund <u>over 50 Silicon Valley startups</u>. [310] Plus he claimed TiE helped entrepreneurs get <u>$75 billion in venture capital</u>. [332]

"Mafia" got Unjustified Venture Capital

Many US venture capital firms also favored members of the Indian "Mafia." For example, a partner in the New Enterprise Associates venture capital firm revealed in 2000 that _almost all of the venture deals in his company's portfolio had some connection to TiE_. And, almost half of the companies in its venture capital portfolio had a CEO who was involved in TiE. [312]

They even got venture capital from major US corporations. (Also see Java fund)

And, they got money from our Department of Defense and other US government agencies. (Also see Defense funding Indian startups.)

An estimated _40% of Silicon Valley startups were "Indian-spawned"_ and IIT graduates accounted for about half of these startups. [303]

Indian "Mafia" Secret Money Source the Middle East?

A Saudi Prince who bought shares in our media also invested in InfoSpace founded by an immigrant from India. [267] The Carlyle Group was reported to have Indians in its upper management, [377] and Saudi investors. _Carlyle also invested in Silicon Valley startups._ [341]

Recall that Senator Abraham sponsored the 1998 massive H-1B quota increase. This was odd for a couple of reasons:

- _He was a Senator from Michigan (1995 to 2001), yet it was Silicon Valley in California where the push for the H-1B visa originated._ [518]

- _H-1B legislation primarily benefited people of Indian ancestry, but Spencer Abraham was_ the only Arab American in the US Senate.

In 1998 Indian immigrant founded US outsourcing firms Syntel and Mastech "contributed" to Abraham's 2000 reelection campaign. These two outsourcing companies were top employers of H-1Bs. With their help Abraham raised $14.5 million. Yet, constituents decided not to reelect him. [518]

"Amazing Web" = Collaboration or Collusion?

The "Mafia" created an *"amazing web"* that gave a whole new meaning to insider collaboration: *"Indians invest in one another's companies, sit on one another's boards, and hire each other in key jobs."* [289]

Immigrants from India were lauded as *"genius entrepreneurs."* [121] An article, "Those Magnificent Indians in Forbes List," published in 2000, by *indiaexpress.com* proclaimed that immigrants from India have a *"Midas touch,"* and *"weave magic"* in the US with their superior genius for creating wealth. [304] One big advantage they claimed that they could hire workers faster and cheaper from a *"pool of Indian engineers."* [331] *"By the mid 1990s... the H-1B program became a conduit for computer programmers and engineers, mainly from India and Taiwan."* [42]

The H-1B legislation, venture capital funding, and media coverage created an illusion of genius. *It does not take a genius to start a company when there are pre-established channels for hiring low cost visa workers, and there are venture funds designated for immigrant startups. Nor does it take a genius to generate revenues when the network has people in US corporations to guarantee customer sales.* [345]

Unjustified Minority Benefits

Rekhi complained of US discrimination. So let's compare India. In 2006, students in India protested affirmative action allowing lower caste Indians, 80% of India's population, to get 49.5% of government run hospital jobs. Police had to use water cannons and batons to subdue protestors. [581] In a 1999, article, "Jessie Jackson is Blowing Smoke, Says TiE's Rekhi," Rekhi wanted Jackson to know that Silicon Valley jobs went to Indian H-1Bs because they were well educated: *"In Silicon Valley especially, it is all merit driven. It is how smart you are."* [467]

However, in 2001 Tony Brown wrote, "Why Indian H-1Bs Are Not Superior and Aframericans Are Not Cry Babies." He pointed to research that uncovered a lucrative illegal industry based in India that was *falsifying resumes and flooding unqualified H-1Bs to staff immigrant founded outsourcing "body shops."* [720]

Shareholder Lawsuits

"Dot Conned and the American Way," a 2005 article reported that in March 2000, InfoSpace stock *plummeted from $260 a share to less than a dollar a share*. A federal judge in Seattle ruled that Infospace founder Naveen Jain had broken insider-trading laws. *The author was astounded when the SEC instead of pursing Jain came to his defense. He asked "What's going on here?"* [293] Infospace denied any wrongdoing. Later, a 2009, article, "Supreme Court Turns Down Appeal From InfoSpace Founder," noted: *"Jain claimed InfoSpace would become the first company worth a trillion dollars, but it lost more than $30 billion in shareholder value during the dotcom bust and Jain was fired in 2002."* [753]

"Ex-Computer Associates CEO Kumar Indicted," a 2004 article reported a *multibillion dollar accounting scandal*: *"Three executives, including Kumar, split stock bonuses worth $1.1 billion in 1998."* And: *"The SEC said that during the company's 2000 fiscal year, Computer Associates "prematurely recognized" more than $1.4 billion in revenue from at least 116 contracts that had not yet been signed."* [297] Sanjay Kumar denied the charges. Three former lower level executives "entered guilty pleas" and cooperated with prosecutors, *"the company agreed to pay $225 million to shareholders in a settlement that allows it to defer criminal prosecution."* [297]

A 2004 article, "i2 Settles Class Action and Derivative Lawsuits," reported that an $84 million settlement was reached. Company insurance paid $43 million, Sanjiv Sidhu, i2's CEO agreed to buy $20 million in common stock, and i2 paid the rest. The Defendants, *i2 and its directors and officers, admitted no wrongdoing.* [421] (Note: In 2002, Enron's Ken Lay resigned from i2's board.) [298]

Where is Justice for Americans?

Did the US corporations who bought their startups and the US citizens who bought their stock get a good deal, or did Americans get scammed on a scale that is hard to fathom? While there were some lawsuits and settlements, most Americans are still waiting for justice.

Chapter 19

Target "Upper Echelons"

Corporate America

Who's at the helm steering our county off course?

The prime target of the Indian "Mafia" was Corporate America: *"The Indian network works well, especially because the larger companies like Sun, Oracle, and HP have a large number of Indians,"* wrote AnnaLee Saxenian. [372] In her May 2000, "Silicon Valley's New Immigrant Entrepreneurs" Working Paper she lauds how ethnic networks opened doors for immigrant entrepreneurs. Saxenian included a quote from Moham Trika, CEO of inXight a venture startup within Xerox that gave an eye-opening revelation into how immigrant entrepreneurs got wealthy. The key is inside access to confidential information:

> *"Your ability to manage risk is improved by these networks. ... I can approach literally any big company, or any company in the Bay Area, and find two or three contacts ... through the TiE network I know so-and-so in Oracle, etc. ... <u>every major software company or any software company must have at least two or three Indians or Chinese in there ... And because they are there, it is very easy for me</u>, or my technical officer, to create that bond, to pick up the phone and say: Swaminathan, can you help me, can you tell me what's going on ... <u>he'll say don't quote me</u> but the decisions is because of this, this and this. Based on this you can reformulate your strategy, your pricing, or your offer ... **<u>Such contacts are critical for startups</u>**." [372]*

India "Breeding American Business Leaders"?

"WHIZ KIDS, *The Indian Institute of Technology is Breeding American Business Leaders from Silicon Valley to Wall St.*" was the incredulous title of the November 25, 1998, *BusinessWeek*'s cover story [303] Does America need India to "*breed*" our leaders? Imagine the reaction in India if they were taxed to educate American youth, and we claimed that Americans were breeding the future leaders of India.

The cover pictured IIT students as the "*hottest export India has ever produced.*" It called IIT a "*star factory.*" And said IIT graduates had a "*leg up on American students*" in "*technical brilliance*" and "*management skills.*" Taking American jobs made them "*highly prized in India's contractual marriage market.*" [303] However, the article contradicts its bold claims. It said IIT graduates anxiously seek acceptance into US universities. Why? Because IIT students "*know that an advanced degree from a U.S. institution is the entry ticket to an American or global corporation.*" It failed to mention foreign students receive *non-immigrant visas, and were taking tax funded aid that should have gone to young Americans.*

Disturbingly, *BusinessWeek* ran this story *just six months after India's nuclear bomb test that caught our government off guard and resulted in US sanctions against India.* Did IIT graduate Vasant Prabhu, *President of the Information and Media Services for The McGraw-Hill Companies* the parent company of *BusinessWeek*, play a role in getting this IIT cover story? [366]

IIT graduates surpassed all other Asians in obtaining jobs in the "*upper echelons*" of Corporate America. The article said: "*IIT grads in the U.S. have been formalizing their powerful network.*" India's strategy was for IIT graduates to follow the example of Taiwan by seeking executive positions in American Corporations that they could then exploit *to* "*set up ventures in their native country*" *and to* "*play a key role in the resurgence of India,*" The article lauded "*the rise of the IITians*": *Kanwal Rekhi, Vinod Khosla, Rajat Gupta (McKinsey), Victor J. Menezes (Citigroup), Rakesh Gangwal (President of US Airways), and many more...* [303]

Penetrated Upper Echelons of American Corporations

"We are known as the Indian Mafia. We are the wealthiest among all ethnic groups in America, even faring better than the whites and the natives." A 2000 article, "Proud to be an Indian" said immigrants from India were upper level managers in big American corporations including: *Arthur Anderson, United Airlines, US Air, CitiBank, Providian, and Bell Labs.* [192] It said Rajat Gupta head of McKinsey was advising big multinationals *"on how to run their business."* [192] It listed the following companies:

Indians Penetrated Upper Management in US Companies	
Government contractors	The Carlyle Group, General Dynamics Corporation, Litton PRC, Lucent Technologies, Motorola, Raytheon, ...
Mortgage	Fannie Mae, Freddie Mac, ...
Financial	Venture Fund, Columbia Capital, ...
Internet	Network Solutions, America Online, Cybercash, The Motley Fool, ...
Telecom	MCI WorldCom, Nextel Communications, Bell Atlantic
High tech	Hughes Network Systems, MicroStrategy, Teligent, MindBank, DynCorp, Consumer Elec. Assoc, Draper Atlantic, Spacevest, ...
Airline	US Airways, United Airlines CIENA Corp,
Consulting	Computer Associates, SAIC, ...
Healthcare	INOVA, and more ... [377]

Updated in 2002, "Proud to be an Indian" claimed that by 2025, India planned to emerge as a *"superpower in IT & Medical research."* [377]

The managing director for Sun Microsystems India in 2001 explained their network deal making: *You put money in their bank accounts so they have money to buy from your company.* An example: *"Sun is one of Citibank's top clients ... and Citibank happens to be Sun India's largest customer."* [118]

The IIT-ians in 2004 claimed that large numbers of IIT graduates had strategically penetrated the *executive ranks* of our high tech industry such as *NASA, Microsoft, IBM, Bell Labs,* financial industry such as *Kleiner Perkins, Citigroup, International Money Fund (IMF),* consulting industry such as McKinsey, and our media industry. [190]

Vinod Khosla–KPCB Venture Capital

Vinod Khosla was the *"wealthiest Indian in the Valley,"* reported a 2000 *Fortune* article, "The Indians of Silicon Valley." [289] Khosla, like Rekhi, is an IIT graduate and co-founder of TiE. He came to the US as a graduate student to study at Carnegie Mellon. [323] Unlike most in the India "Mafia" that keep low profiles, he sought publicity.

Khosla co-founded Sun Microsystems in 1982 along with Scott McNealy, Andy Bechtolsheim, and Bill Joy.

In 1986, Khosla joined venture capital firm Kleiner, Perkins, Caufield & Byers (KPCB) where he became a managing partner. [312] [188] Five years later, in 2001, KPCB revealed that *"40% of its portfolio consists of companies founded or managed by people of Indian origin."* This is especially significant because KPCB was one of the biggest venture capital firms in Silicon Valley. [187] *Demographically, India diaspora made up less than 1% of our population yet they got 40% of the KPCB deals. That's **40 times their fair share!**KPCB even sponsored TiE's annual conference.*

Through KPCB, Khosla obtained positions on the boards of many high-tech startups such as:

- *QWEST Communications, Corvis Corporation, Juniper Networks, Siara Systems, Asera, Concentric Network, Corio Inc., Doublebill.com, Coreon Inc, Broadband Office Surmodics.*[188]

A 2000, *IndoLink* article, "Silicon Spice Acquired by Broadcom for $1.2 Billion," said Khosla was involved in big deals such as:

- *Cisco's $6.9 billion acquisition of Cerent, (KPCB provided venture capital to Silicon Spice and Cisco was a customer of Silicon Spice.)*
- *Redback Networks' $4.3 billion acquisition of Siara.* [390]

Investing in a company and then buying from that company guarantees sales. In fact, buying from a company invested in could be done to manipulate financial statements to make a company appear more valuable to the public than it really is.

Java Fund for Dotcom Startups Skyrocketed Sun

How much money did you invest in dotcoms? It may be more than you know. The level of venture capital investment linked to Java, Sun Microsystems's software for creating internet programs and other applications, was stupefying.

A $100 million Java Fund for dotcom startups was funded by ten corporations! KPCB announced in August 1996, that it partnered with: *Sun Microsystems (Vinod Khosla co-founded)*, Cisco, Comcast, Compaq, IBM, Itochu, Netscape, Oracle, Tele-Communications, and US West Media Group to form the fund. The contributions were approximately: KPCB $30 million, Sun $15 million and the other companies' ranged from $4 million to $7 million each. [432] [431]

A Sun Microsystems VP estimated that 70% of the company's growth in 1999-2000 came from the dotcom boom. [117] Did the Java Fund *put money in startups bank accounts* so they could buy from Sun and manipulate Sun Microsystems stock to make the company appear *"wildly successful"*? A failing Sun Microsystems was acquired by Oracle in 2009. How many insiders got rich during the wild dotcom ride?

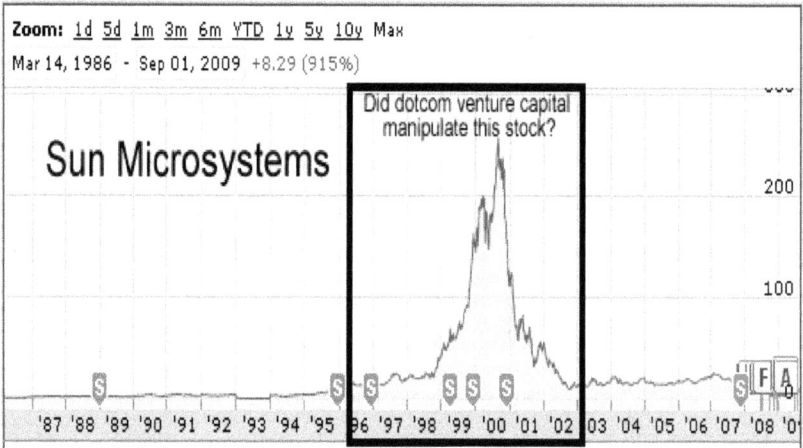

Zoom: 1d 5d 1m 3m 6m YTD 1y 5y 10y Max
Mar 14, 1986 - Sep 01, 2009 +8.29 (915%)

Did dotcom venture capital manipulate this stock?

Sun Microsystems

The year 1996, when the Java Fund was formed, was a pivotal year in setting the stage for India's run on US high tech worker visas and the US dotcom stock market. In the first two quarters of 1996, more venture capital money flowed into the US software industry than to any other industry sector. And, there were other Java funds fueling the dotcom boom. For example, in 1996, venture capital firm Bessemer Venture Partners became involved in funding Java startups.

So, money Americans invested in large US corporations was used as a source of venture capital to fund startups. Did immigrants from India in the upper management of US corporations misdirect corporate funds to provide venture capital such as the Java Fund to Indian startups? Were executives in the US corporations providing the venture capital conspiring with startups to inflate sales and stock values through reciprocal purchasing?

US Stock Market Circle of Deception

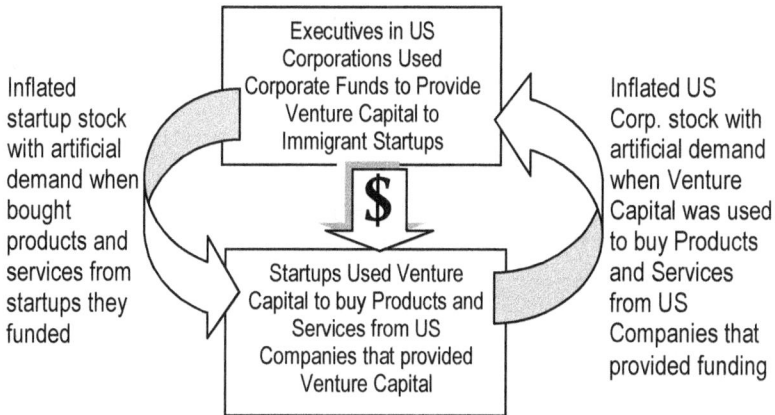

Inflated startup stock with artificial demand when bought products and services from startups they funded

Executives in US Corporations Used Corporate Funds to Provide Venture Capital to Immigrant Startups

$

Startups Used Venture Capital to buy Products and Services from US Companies that provided Venture Capital

Inflated US Corp. stock with artificial demand when Venture Capital was used to buy Products and Services from US Companies that provided funding

"Mafia" Upper Echelons US Job & Technology Transfer

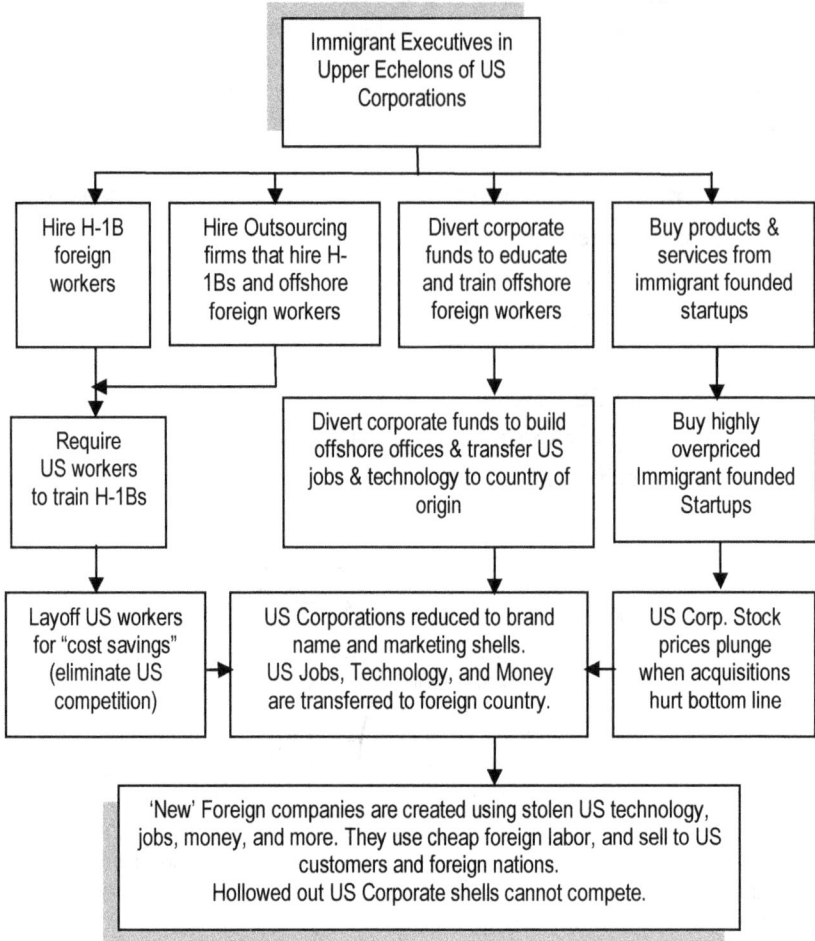

```
                    ┌─────────────────────┐
                    │ Immigrant Executives│
                    │  in Upper Echelons  │
                    │   of US Corporations│
                    └─────────────────────┘
```

| Hire H-1B foreign workers | Hire Outsourcing firms that hire H-1Bs and offshore foreign workers | Divert corporate funds to educate and train offshore foreign workers | Buy products & services from immigrant founded startups |

| Require US workers to train H-1Bs | Divert corporate funds to build offshore offices & transfer US jobs & technology to country of origin | Buy highly overpriced Immigrant founded Startups |

| Layoff US workers for "cost savings" (eliminate US competition) | US Corporations reduced to brand name and marketing shells. US Jobs, Technology, and Money are transferred to foreign country. | US Corp. Stock prices plunge when acquisitions hurt bottom line |

'New' Foreign companies are created using stolen US technology, jobs, money, and more. They use cheap foreign labor, and sell to US customers and foreign nations. Hollowed out US Corporate shells cannot compete.

"OUSTED" INDIAN CEO'S

According to a 2001 article, some US CEOs who were born in India were "ousted" from the US corporations where they had risen to power. Rana Talwar CEO left Standard Chartered plc. And, Rakesh Ganwal left US Airways following a third quarter loss of $766 million. However, Rono Dutta remained as president and COO at US Airways despite the huge losses. [366]

Indian Immigrants Sold Startups to US Corporations

Executives were gambling with stockholders' investments, and employees' jobs. Acquisitions and mergers create an opportunity for executives to manipulate financial statements to take bonuses. The companies rarely benefit. *"More than two-thirds of all mergers fail."* [354]

Dozens of people from the India network penetrated the executive ranks of US telecom blue chip corporations including *AT&T, Bell, Lucent, Cisco, and Qualcomm* claimed a July 2000 *indiaexpress.com* article, "Wireless Whisper: Design Network Begins to Takeover Telecom World." Did they misuse their positions to get US corporations to acquire India immigrant founded telecom companies?

In the 1990's people from India started several network and telecom companies that at the peak of the dotcom boom had stock priced at over $100 billion! A few of the startups listed included:

- *Nexabit Networks, Stratumone, Tachion, Qlogic, Juniper Networks, Cerent, Sycamore Networks, Exodus Communications, Brocade Communications, Cobalt Networks InteliNet Technologies, and Accelerated Networks.*

In 1996, Lucent paid an astounding ***$900 million for Nexabit, founded by Mukesh Chatter, even though the company had no revenues!*** This was part of a pattern: *"In at least half a dozen cases, the Indian founders have <u>sold their companies to giant conglomerates for fortunes in excess of $500 million</u>."* [244] Did US companies pay grossly inflated prices for acquisitions that had little or no real value?

There were an estimated 2,000 startups in Silicon Valley in 2002, the network again claimed that *"40% are Indian spawned."* [331] IIT graduates founded half of these Indian startups. The VP of distribution channels for Cisco was from India. He and his friends *keep a low profile preferring to remain anonymous.* He claimed all his friends worked in high tech jobs and *almost all have sold a startup to a large American corporation.* [289] Interestingly, Juniper networks, an Indian startup, was said to be "the greatest threat to Cisco." [331]

Raj Singh Sold Three Startups for $11 Billion!

Raj Singh sold three startups to US companies for $11 billion in 1999! To put this in perspective the total US trade with India ran $11 billion. Cisco, which had immigrants from India in its upper management, bought two of his startups:

- *Cisco paid $6.2 billion for his optical transport startup Cerent. The amount paid **shocked the industry.***
- *Cisco paid about $435 million for his chip startup StratumOne. A record setting price—**two to four times the amount normally paid.***

  Another deal:

- *Redback Networks paid **4.3 billion** for his Siara Networks startup.* [357]

While taking billions in these unprecedented deals, Singh *kept a low profile.* To most Americans he was *"virtually unknown."* [330] How many Americans were harmed by these deals?

So, who is Singh? In the 1960's he got an engineering degree in India where he struggled and found little success. In 1980, he was granted a student visa to the University of Minnesota. Once he had his Master's degree in computer science, he moved to Silicon Valley. He got an entry level job at National Semiconductor. For the next fifteen years he jumped from job to job in the US. Then he met Suhas Patil, *a charter member of TiE* who became his mentor. Vinod Khosla, also *a charter member of TiE*, helped Singh get venture capital to launch a startup named Fiberlane. Khosla sat on the board of directors for Fiberlane which spun off and sold Cerent and Siara. [357]

Singh took the money from selling his three startups, and partnered with Raj Parekh, *a charter member of TiE*, to create the venture capital firm Redwood Ventures Partners. In 1999, Redwood funded over 40 startups. He began to travel around the world *"fixing business deals."* In 1999, Singh was *on the board of 23 companies.* Most were in Silicon Valley, however, others were overseas. In addition Singh planned to *fund education in India.* [357]

Chapter 20

Dotcom Money Educated

Offshore Workers

Pre-dotcom: Money from our technology advances funded our Universities.

Post-dotcom: Money from our technology funded Universities in India.

Now we can answer the question of why India was able to leapfrog and make a generational leap in education that was historically unprecedented.

"India Schools Cash In on Silicon Valley Wealth," a May 2000 article, told how money taken from the US during the dotcom boom went to fund schools in India. [360] *These schools were essential to NRIs planning to offshore our professional jobs to India.*

Following the dotcom crash, TiE's website talked about giving back to the community. This sounds good until you realize by "community" they mean people from India and the Indus region. Not, the United States where they got an education at our expense and were granted US citizenship. [319]

India's diaspora in our country wanted to help *"their country."* They were working with institutes of higher education in India in 2003 to *"scout, mentor and incubate talent in India to create entrepreneurs."* [319] Moreover using our Silicon Valley as a base, TiE branched out to form *a global TiE network* comprised of 800 Charter members plus 8,000 regular members. [512] [333]

Rekhi's Offshore "vision" Funding Incubators

Kanwal Rekhi's "vision" while pumping the dotcom bubble in the US was *to finance incubators in India to spawn startups selling: "routing technology, information security, robotics, business activity monitoring, electronic design automation, and decision support systems for financial institutions."* [190] These were the same US technologies that India diaspora were entrusted by our corporations to provide outsourcing services.

So, prior to the dotcom crash in America, Rekhi was positioning India to exploit the crash. He and Nandan Nilekhani financed the Kanwal Rekhi School of Information Technology (KReSIT) to train IT leaders in India in a preparation for a major IT industry growth boom. [349] KReSIT opened its doors in Bombay India in July 1999. Everything was now ready for massive offshoring by US corporations. The dotcom crash happened just in time to feed the jobs that India was ready and waiting for.

Following the dotcom crash, in 2001, Rekhi began traveling to India every other month. [350]

Rekhi—Raising Money for India's IIT

Also, in 1999, Kanwal Rekhi and Mr. Nandan, the president of Infosys, raised money to turn India's IIT into a world class university. They funded research in *bio-sciences, bio-engineering, nanotechnology, and more.* Rekhi and Nandan claimed they were paying back their debt for having gotten a free education at IIT. In their own words: *"The IIT is generating funds by working on technology transfer and consultancy projects."* [315] This quote links consulting with US technology transfer.

Rekhi led a group of thirteen Indian immigrant Silicon Valley CEOs on a trip back to India in December 1999 to meet with the Prime Minister. All these CEOs were *IIT graduates who became rich during the US dotcom boom.* They planned to raise $1 billion for IIT. *Although they represented their "contributions" as philanthropic, some government leaders in India were concerned that they had ulterior motives to take control of India's state assets.* [360] Why did they not trust them?

Dotcom Money Built Education Centers in India

Another group of Indian immigrants led by Purnendu Chatterjee, managing director of the Chatterjee Group based in New York, raised money to pay for advanced degree educational centers in India. *Their long term goal was to create a Silicon Valley type technology environment that would make India a superpower.* One of these immigrants, K.B. Chandrasekhar felt that India could accomplish a superpower status by *intellectual competition.* [360] Is he a US citizen?

Dotcom Money Built Indian School of Business (ISB)

"Hyderabad's Harvard: A University Built on an Arid Plain with Funds from Overseas Indians...," a 2002 article revealed that $75 million of overseas money *i.e. dotcom money from the US*, was spent to build the Indian School of Business (ISB). The school in Hyderabad opened in July 2001. Major contributors included <u>Kanwal Rekhi</u>, K.B. Chandrasekhar, B.V. Jagadeesh, and Romesh Wadhwani. McKinsey, Citibank and HSBC provided scholarships for ISB.

*ISB was conceived by **Rajat Gupta** while advising US corporations as a managing partner of McKinsey. His goal was for ISB to compete against US universities such as Harvard and Wharton.* Disturbingly the faculties of our universities–*Wharton and Northwestern University's Kellogg School of Management helped develop* the ISB curriculum and took teaching stints in India. ISB recruited its faculty from our universities. A McKinsey consultant, Pramath Sinha, was the school's dean until June 2002. McKinsey and Lehman Brothers recruited from ISB. Graduates *who got jobs in the US were paid about $80,000 a year while those in India only got about $17,000.* [492]

Heritage Fund to Finance Education and Research

TiE was also building a global network of "IIT-ians." As part of this strategy, in 2002, The Heritage Fund was created to help finance student research and education at IIT Bombay. [361]

Chapter 21

"Mafia" Exploits US Economic

Downturn & War

In his farewell address George Washington warned that "corrupt" citizens who favor a foreign nation may "betray or sacrifice the interests of their own country."

India used the economic downturn caused by the dotcom crash and the war to push for US corporations to dramatically accelerate offshoring. Not only was India going after our programming jobs, India wanted US corporations to set up research centers in India, and for US venture capital to fund startups based in India. [6]

The forces behind the dotcom crash pressured American companies to offshore under the guise that it would help them survive the impact of the dotcom crash. This was taking American corporations down a self destructive path. To revive US corporations, and the US economy, *the strategy needed was to cut outsourcing and offshoring, not accelerate and expand it.* [299]

"U.S. Firms Move IT Overseas," a 2002 CNET *News.com* report, said that American IT service providers were *compelled to send service jobs overseas because of Indian outsourcing firms operating in the US*. [102] Why? Because some Indian firms selling IT services in the United States sent *90% to 95% of the work offshore to low paid workers in India. This put 40% to 50% of American IT service jobs at risk of being lost to overseas competition by 2012.* [102] Our government did nothing to stop this.

"Reshaping Corporate America"!

"The Rise of India: Growth is just starting, but the country's brainpower is already *__reshaping Corporate America__*" a 2003 BusinessWeek cover story *proclaimed. It found the <u>chief architects behind the offshoring US R&D business model were 30,000 Indian diaspora who worked in Silicon Valley at major US chip and software companies</u>.* They persuaded companies such as Intel, Cisco, and Oracle, *to build offshore research labs in India.* [300] A subtitle, "Brainpower India and Silicon Valley: Now the R&D Flows Both Ways," featured Kanwal Rekhi who credited offshoring to India with saving US companies from *"oblivion."* [300]

- *By 2002, US companies, including: Oracle, IBM, Sun Microsystems, Cisco, and Microsoft, had spent about <u>$10 billion expanding offshore operations in India claiming it would cut costs</u>. [175] Oracle expanded its Technology Park in Bangalore by building a 213,000 square foot facility complete with an 11 story parking garage, recreation center, onsite cafeteria, and a fully stocked library. [175]*

- *US corporations including: Cisco, Siemens, Lucent, TI, and Alcatel provided money, technology, and training to create offshore R&D development centers in India. This was a big change because previously offshored jobs were the lower skill jobs. Another big change was that <u>India no longer felt a need to keep a low profile cloaking US offshoring with secrecy and working anonymously</u>. [378]*

- *"India to See R&D Outsourcing Boom" a 2004 article said India was launching a national initiative targeting strategic US technologies for outsourcing ranging from semiconductors, to micro-electronics, to nanotechnology. The article <u>acknowledged some resistance to India taking over this R&D through outsourcing contracts due to low levels of expertise, risks of intellectual property theft, and the risk of instability in the R&D facilities</u>. [119]*

"India's Outsourcers Gain Traction," a 2004 article, said Infosys, Wipro, and Satyam *"compete head-on with IBM, Accenture, EDS, and others."* They met onsite with US customer contacts, and then, often without the customers' knowledge, channeled the work offshore to India. [587]

Advising US Companies "Vital for Profits" to Offshore

When a New Jersey Senator tried to get a bill passed in 2003 that would require state government work be done in the US, India went running to–Kanwal Rekhi for advice. [586] An *indiacurrents.com* article, "Growing Partnership: Major US Companies are Setting Up Offices in India for Software Development," reported Rekhi said offshoring US government jobs was "problematic," but it was easier to offshore our commercial jobs.

Rekhi claimed that offshoring jobs to India would cut costs more than 50%. He said, "America was not producing enough software engineers to start with." And he argued that it was more economical to send the work to India (offshore) than to import H-1Bs. Rekhi said, "Outsourcing to India will enable us to do the jobs that no American will do at the wages Indians are paid." [586] Notice Rekhi used "*us*" referring to himself not as an American, but as an Indian. This article connects the dots. It traces the source of the US "cost savings" and "worker shortage" claims to the Indian "Mafia"; and exposes *they were hidden key agents behind offshoring our jobs to India.*

The Sand Hill Group sponsored an Offshoring Conference in California in 2003 where it *decreed that offshoring software development was "vital for profits" because of the downturn in the US economy.* Madhavan Rangaswami co-founded this group that reported, "*more than 8 in 10 software companies are now shipping work overseas or plan to do so in the next year.*" He noted that offshoring was a contentious topic in the US where *offshoring caused high tech unemployment and jeopardized US technological leadership.* [113] Yet, Rangaswami said US executives were *not worried about intellectual property risks inherent in offshoring.* [84]

In 2005, Rangaswami continued to advise software companies "*must take development offshore*" to generate margin for investors. Surprisingly, his dual role as an advisor to Aspect Development and i2 Technologies was still listed in his expert advisor credentials. [455] After *i2 acquired Aspect for $9 billion*, the stock fell like a rock *causing one of the worst dotcom crashes.*

Most Dismal Stock Market in 200 Year History!

Recall in the first chapter that Jim Tankersley said that technology advancements and international markets paid off for American companies but not for American workers. [972]

However, accounting tricks just made it look like it paid off for a short while. *"Since End of 1999, U.S. Stocks' Performance Has Been the All-Time Clunker, Even 1930s Beat It,"* a *Wall Street Journal* analysis found in 2009. It said investors would have done better putting their money *"under a mattress."* Notice the timeline started with the dotcom fiasco. Shockingly the WSJ found: *"In nearly 200 years of recorded stock market history, no calendar decade has seen such a dismal performance as the 2000s."* [1017]

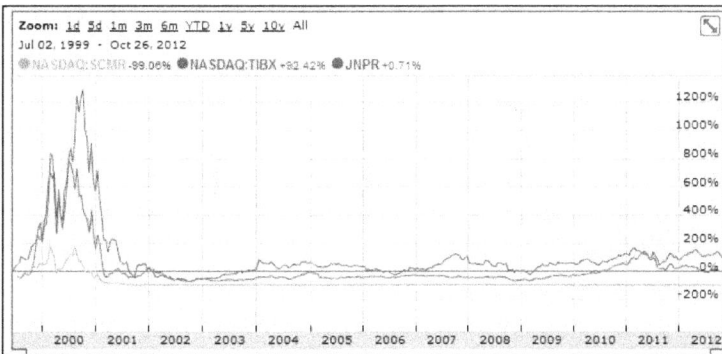

Above is an update of the earlier stock performance chart.

A few people got filthy rich extracting millions and even billions of dollars from our stock market. As a nation, we value and reward people based on performance. However, what did they do to merit taking millions or billions out of our stock market. What has gone on here is clearly wrong and not based on performance. The American public was fleeced. Millions of Americans lost money that they had worked for years to earn. Money they needed for college, or to buy a home, or for retirement. Our justice system ought to resolve this huge injustice against Americans.

TiE Rolling in Dough and Deals After Dotcom Crash

Just months after our terrible multi-trillion dollar dotcom crash, *TiE members hobnobbing at the Santa Clara Marriott were referred to as a "room full of billionaires."*– *"The recent dot-com implosions and falling tech stocks notwithstanding, this bland conference room is burning with entrepreneurial spirit."* A *SiliconValley.com*: Special Report, "The TiE That Binds," featured a picture of Rekhi being *"treated like a movie star by aspiring young entrepreneurs."* It said Indian owned companies in Silicon Valley were important to "the home country" because *they recruited visa workers and brought business to India.* [463]

TiE members had gotten rich selling startups. The most revered was Kanwal Rekhi who they said had $250 million. And in turn, Rekhi claimed that he knew about 30 more Indians that had as much or more money than he did. [463]

Rekhi was "horrified" when a wannabe Indian entrepreneur put in his own money. Rekhi said he should get *"other people's money."* The wannabe told Rekhi that *"several of his Indian friends were on board ... but they have visa problems."* Rekhi responded: *"Those are not the kind of people you need! You need mainline, quality people! You need whiteys!"* [463]

Many of the people getting rich helping launch TiE startups were "whiteys." For example a 2000, *Fortune* article, "The Indians of Silicon Valley," wrote that, *"construction executive Ed Shay and venture capitalist John Doughery, who have since (1995 to 2000) invested in almost every one of Rekhi's deals."* [289] How many "whiteys" investing in TiE startups were executives in big American corporations?

Recall Duke Professor Vivek Wadhwa' 2007 study talked about how earlier studies focused on "contributions" of immigrants who founded dotcoms. [687]

While America was reeling from the April 2000 dotcom crash, TiE members were ready to spin-off more startups and IPOs. [312] They were holding meetings and conferences and talking about the money they made during the dotcom boom.

TiE Reciprocity

The Indian "Mafia" feeds on reciprocity.

"*As in all good networks, reciprocity keeps the wheels turning*," wrote Melanie Warner about "The Indians of Silicon Valley," in the May issue of *Fortune*. As an example she quoted K.B. Chandrasekhar (Chandra) who said: "*I always make sure Kanwal gets a good deal.*" [289]

Warner provided *a rare inside glimpse into their exclusive deal making* by telling about deals connected to a web service company Impresse:

- "*Chandra got to do something virtually every investor in the Valley would kill to do—he invested alongside Kleiner Perkins and Benchmark.*"

- "*Rekhi, because he's the godfather and everyone wants him to invest, also got in on the deal.*" [289]

- And *Satish Gupta, CEO of Cradle Technologies got in on the deal because the CEO of Impresse was an angel investor in his company.* [289]

Siliconindia "A Very Exclusive Club"

Siliconindia claimed to be "*a very exclusive club*" that brings together the "*Asian Indian community*," on its website in 2001. It held an Investor Entrepreneur Forum at its Annual Conference. *Technology workers, entrepreneurs, venture capitalists, and academics from around the world met to* "*exchange ideas, network, and cut deals.*" [306]

At the conference, "*selected companies*" gained an audience with high profile Silicon Valley venture capitalists, met with *key business contacts*, recruited employees for the startups (H-1Bs?), and *found customers*. This exclusive club said *Siliconindia* provided members with advantages that gave them "*greater traction in the market from all perspectives.*" [306]

Note: they came to Silicon Valley, USA, but their website was titled *Siliconindia.com*.

They published a *siliconindia* magazine that had a circulation of 60,000 readers. [312]

TiE Promotes India Startups

Kanwal Rekhi, President of TiE, was the first of 20 speakers listed for a 2000 TiE Conference held in Bangalore India after the dotcom crash. The conference brochure said Rekhi was *seeking recognition for India's universities, and gave $2 million to IIT for a new Information Technology school.* [469] *(Was there a connection to US House Resolution 227 recognizing IITs sponsored by Bobby Jindal in 2005.)*

Another speaker, Poornima Jairaj, a *charter member of TiE*, was a partner with Global Technology Ventures founded a month after the crash. They were *preparing a 59 acre business incubator park in Bangalore,* and planned to provide *money, management teams, and legal advice to quickly launch technology startups in India.* [469]

Other speakers at this 2000 conference in India included:

■   *AnnaLee Saxenian the author of studies used to promote outsourcing to US business and US government agencies.*

■   *Subroto Bagchi, CEO of Mindtree Consulting, who helped get India's software industry started by setting up Wipro in Silicon Valley.*

■   *Dewang Mehta, President of NASSCOM, who organized 100 seminars to lobby our government, and other governments to outsource to India.*

■   *Atul Vashistha, CEO of neoIT, who sold BPO to US companies.*

■   *Nandan Nilekani, cofounder of NASSCOM, and on India's Securities and Exchange Board.*

■   *Alex Lightman, whose book America Inc. "addresses the feasibility of running the United States as a publicly owned company."*

■   *Raj Popli a TiE Charter member who managed a Silicon Valley fund that helped launch 40 technology startups ... many of which had IPOs.*

■   *Sridhar Mitta who set up Wipro's R&D division that sold outsourced R&D services to Cisco, Lucent, Sun Microsystems, Alltel, ...*

■   *Sridhar Iyengar, Charter member of TiE, a KPMG partner who led India operations increasing business in India by 400%.* [469]

How many of these speakers were US citizens?

"India-centric" Plan Required for US Startups

While our economy was suffering, members of the Indian "Mafia" had millions to invest. *"That Indian-promoted companies account for the biggest chunk of Silicon Valley start-ups is not new."* [378]

"A global telecom civilization is taking shape. ... a new Valley is coming up. Call it the New Indus Valley ..." wrote Shyamanuja Das in his "TECH START-UPS: Indus Valley," 2002 article in the *CIOL Cybertimes.* [378]

Because US companies displaced Americans with H-1Bs, India had a lot of 30-45 year olds living in the US ready to become entrepreneurs. Many had jobs that allowed them to go on frequent trips to India where they developed business contacts. In September 2002, it was reported that Silicon Valley "is *today full with start-ups which have at least one Indian member in the core team."* [378] Has their portion of US startups now exceeded 40%?

The *new "India-US model"* startups were incorporated in America like the dotcoms; however, now *venture capital funding was contingent on an "India-centric" business plan. Venture funding required US startups' high tech product development work be offshored to India.* [378]

Beyond getting development work from startups, India's biggest win by far was *the recent trend for multinationals i.e. American corporations to fully outsource product development. American corporations were building development centers in India, and they were outsourcing development to Wipro, HCL or other Indian companies.* [378]

Forbes wondered how during our economic downturn India had such success according to a 2003, Hindustantimes.com: "Eighteen Indian Companies in Forbes List," of successful companies outside the United States. [320] *That's easy to explain, for example, at least 3 of the IT companies listed became rich offshoring US jobs—Wipro, Infosys, and Satyam.* India was taking our jobs, money, and research opportunities by luring US corporations to offshore.

US Money Funds Startups Based in India

Another major change in 2002, was that _Silicon Valley venture capital firms favored funding startups headquartered in India instead of the United States!_ The intent here was to create a "Silicon Valley" in India. [378]

This "_new breed" of startups_ was formed by people in India who had R&D experience from working in our high tech corporations. They were tasked with helping _India create its own intellectual property._ India planned to lock up customer service for any technology they developed. Deals were already being made with China and Hong Kong. [378]

"Private Equity Pours Into India," a 2005 _BusinessWeek_ article by Manjeet Kripalani, reported _large US equity companies such as Carlyle (a US military contractor) and the Blackstone Group were channeling money to India funding startups in high tech outsourcing. One big target was the US pharmaceutical industry._ After hiring McKinsey & Co. for consulting advice, Blackstone decided to invest $1 billion in India. [721]

Three Indians were _in the top_ 10 of Forbes' top 100 venture capitalists list for 2005 including: _Ram Shriram, Vinod Khosla, and Pramod Haque._ [189]

"Kanwal Rekhi Raising $150-$175 Million India-specific Fund," a 2006 announcement on _VC Circle_ told how Rekhi's organization, Inventus Capital Partners, was raising money to invest in _Indian startups_ in Bangalore and Silicon Valley. [602]

TiE was at "_the forefront of promoting venture capital in India_." In 2007 TiE claimed it had spread to 5 continents and had 10,000 members. TiE's members and sponsors ranged "_from venture capital investors, law firms, accounting firms, banks, ..._" [659]

Taking tens to hundreds of billions of dollars out of circulation in our country to fund ventures in India played a significant role in creating our economic crisis.

TiE "Invisible Hand Behind" Deals

"TiE—The Secrets of Success," a 2005 *tie-asia.org* article said TiE is the *"invisible hand behind"* 300 or more startups at any point in time. TiE was over 12 years old, still most Americans did not know this network was operating in our country–TiE is *"the best kept secret."* [604]

"TiE and India are feeding off each other," and "India's economy has skyrocketed," the article said. It credits TiE for India's *"technological emergence."* TiE startups moved into a new phase that required a *split workforce with workers in Silicon Valley and in India*. The article says, *"We've not even begun to see the results of what these folks have begun to put in place over these past several years."* [604] What have they put in place? TiE's tentacles extend from its "California hub" to 9 countries including Pakistan. [604]

TiE's "charter" memberships are by invitation only. TiE *connects entrepreneurs from India with TiE members who are executives in large US corporations, US banks, and US venture capital firms.* A member explained that connections went beyond business ties to *"your mother, your grandmother"* and *ties to India.* Contacts for *"deals and recruitment"* provided an edge, *"The Rolodex is more important than what you know."* [604]

TiE's website in September 2004 boasted that within a 30 day period four of its members sold companies:

- *Matrix (CEO Piyush Sodha) sold for $230 million in cash to Symbol Technologies.*
- *Intelsat (COO Ramu Potarazu) sold for $3 billion to Zeus Holdings.*
- *AC Technologies (CEO Satya Akulawas) sold for $50 million in cash to PEC Solutions*
- *And, DigitalNet Holdings (CEO Ken Bajaj) sold for about $595 million cash to BAE Systems North America.* [592]

Membership in TiE was expanded to include people with business interests in India, Bangladesh, Nepal and Sri Lanka. In 2005, TiE's charter members were 98% IndUS people. [604]

200,000 Indians Became Millionaires in by 2007!

"The Golden Diaspora," by Anthony Spaeth/New Delhi in a 2001 *Time Magazine* article, claimed, "*the Indian diaspora in the U.S. tends to be the intellectual and commercial elite.*" Written less than a year after our devastating dotcom crash, he claimed, "<u>*The number of Indian American New Economy millionaires is in the thousands.*</u>" [187]

Not all the millionaires were in Silicon Valley. For example, Gururaj Despande who lived in Massachusetts was a co-founder of multiple network technology companies and was estimated to have accumulated over $4 billion from his startups. [187]

"*One in every nine Indians in the US is a millionaire, comprising 10% of US millionaires. Source: 2003 Merrill Lynch SA Marketing Study,*" in 2007 according to a Wikipedia article, "Non-resident Indian and Person of Indian Origin." [618] <u>*If this is true, given that NRIs were less than 1% of our population, either NRIs were 9 times more superior than other Americans or something very sinister has been going on under the radar in America.*</u>

"Engineers Learning People Skills," a 2007 *att.net* article said University of California's Berkeley's director of Entrepreneurship & Technology was Professor Ikhlaq Sidhu, and its dean of engineering was S. Shankkar Sastry. Students in the school of engineering were being instructed on how to become entrepreneurs. Students were laughingly taught that independent investors were the three "Fs", meaning *__friends, family, and fools__*. [662] *So Americans who were not in their circle of friends or family were "fools" if they bought stock in their startups. And this was funny?*

By 2007 the number of *__NRI millionaires in the US hit a shocking 200,000__* according to USINPAC's website! [625] How did so many Indians (Sikhs, Hindus, and Muslims), who arrived in America broke, become millionaires? *It appears highly suspect that during the war in Iraq where many young Americans are risking their lives, the Indian "Mafia" network doubled its number of millionaires in America from 100,000 to 200,000.* Were they making money off the war?

Secret Money Source—US Department of Defense!

"Skilled Indian Immigrants Create Wealth for America," an article on *INDOLink.com,*—*"Linking Indians Worldwide"*, was written about Vivek Wadhwa's 2007 Duke study. [685]

A "Related Findings" section *"concluded that Indian immigrants in America account for less than 0.75% of the US population, but their contribution to the U.S. Department of Defense (DoD) research is more than **20 times the population base**."* [685] It said this was *the first time the magnitude of US defense research jobs done by Indians had been quantified.* So, Indian Americans got 20 times their fair share of our sensitive high paying defense research jobs!

Most of the jobs were in academics, i.e. *university professors who hired "younger post-doctoral fellows and graduate students, also of Indian origin, for their research efforts." The research "ranged from homeland security to missile technology, advanced ceramics and munitions ..."* [685]

So professors with roots to India who have an extremely disproportionate share of our college professorships were channeling strategic defense research jobs to Indians especially non-citizen Indian graduate students. Non-Americans should not get any of these jobs. (See also More Dangerous than Terrorists book.)

9 out of 10 New IT Jobs Went to H-1Bs in 2001!

The dotcom crash caused massive layoffs of American IT workers. But acted as a windfall for foreign IT workers. In 2001, *over 500,000 American IT workers were laid off, while the number of foreign H-1B visas issued by our government increased by 70% hitting record levels.* American IT workers vital to our economy and national security were devastated in a job market that denied them jobs [29]

H-1Bs took, "*9 out of every 10 new IT jobs in 2001.*" [43] Young Americans graduating with a degree in IT had little chance of obtaining employment in their field of study.

Rekhi Advised H-1Bs on Expired Visas to Stay Illegally

We deserve an explanation of how there can be an *"Immigrant Support Network"* for H-1Bs on *temporary "non-immigrant"* visas. "Kanwal Rekhi Joins ISN Advisory Borad," a 2001 *India West* report said the Immigrants Support Network (ISN) represented H-1B visa holders. Most ISN members were from India. Rekhi promised ISN members he would use his US political clout to influence our politicians at a 2001 ISN meeting. *ISN's members "knew that when Rekhi speaks, people, especially politicians listen."* [347]

"Kanwal Rekhi Advises Laid-off H-1B Workers Not to Leave," was a 2001 ISN report. It said Rekhi told a group of *laid-off H-1Bs* to stay in the US illegally. Because *based on his 35 years of experience; people who stayed illegally had a better chance of immigrating to the United States* than *those who returned to India.* [348] Were members of the Indian "Mafia" among the illegal aliens granted amnesty in 1986? *Do the dotcom, outsourcing and offshoring which cost Americans millions of jobs all trace back to this amnesty?*

Mafia Pursued "Opinion Forming" US Media

The Indian "Mafia" pursued jobs in strategic *"opinion-forming"* US media such as the *Wall Street Journal*. Several people originally from India became writers and reporters for CNN. [240]

Indians created the *SiliconIndia* and *TechMantra* magazines for "the community," *indian-express.com* reported in 2000. [330] Surprisingly, *SiliconIndia's* Editorial Board members included:

- *"Ashok Trivedi, Desh Deshpande, Jayshree Ullal, KB Chandrashekar, Kanwal Rekhi, Mohanbir Sawhney, NR Narayana Murthy, Radha Basu, Ramesh Jain, Sabeer Bhatia, Vijay Vashee, Vinod Dham, Vinod Khosla, Yogesh Gupta."* [242]

In 2006 TiE complained, *"Not Enough Asian Faces on the Telly?"* [592] TiE wanted more Asian faces on US television in IT and medical roles to promote its superpower goals for taking over our IT and medical industries.

Green Cards to Enable More Indian Startups!

"Free H-1Bs, Free the Economy" blogged Wadhwa in 2009. <u>He wanted our government to grant green cards to over a million H-1Bs</u> including: *"doctors, engineers, scientists, researchers and other skilled workers."* H-1Bs are <u>*"stuck in the same old jobs they had maybe a decade ago*</u> *when they* <u>*entered this country,"*</u> complained Wadhwa. [742] Are they here illegally on expired visas? Many Americans would be happy to fill these jobs.

Wadhwa called Americans *"Xenophobes"* if we objected to granting more green cards. He warned that unless we grant green cards, H-1Bs might return to their "home countries" and compete against the US. He said H-1Bs were discriminated against. To the contrary, in *2001 H-1Bs got nine out of every ten new IT jobs.* Americans were the ones discriminated against. Disturbingly, he mocked the *"silly patents filed with the U.S. Patent Office,"* and *claimed that 25% of US global patents were filed by non-citizens.* [742]

How many patents does he think that displaced unemployed American engineers and scientists can file with no job and no access to many of our research labs? And, what good is a global patent when foreign countries flagrantly violate patent laws?

US law requires that companies must attempt to hire US citizens before they can sponsor foreign workers for permanent residence green cards. [709] We had high unemployment therefore, it was unlikely any jobs could not be filled by Americans.

He said granting H-1Bs green cards would "boost" the US economy. And he lamented *that H-1Bs cannot start companies; but, if granted* <u>*green cards they could form "tens of thousands of startups."*</u> [742]

Recall in his 2007 study Wadhwa tried to persuade the US to grant 500,000 green cards, because from 1995-2005 immigrants founded 52% of Silicon Valley startups and employed 450,000 people. *Note that in two years he doubled the number of green cards he was lobbying for from 500,000 in 2007, to over a million in 2009!*

Let's look at some of their startups' US stock performance.

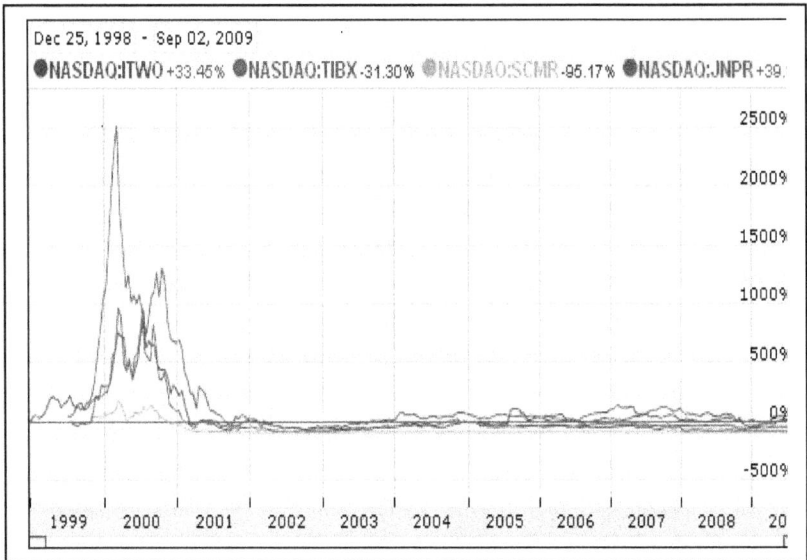

Dec 25, 1998 - Sep 02, 2009
●NASDAQ:ITWO +33.45% ●NASDAQ:TIBX -31.30% ●NASDAQ:SCMR -95.17% ●NASDAQ:JNPR +39.

It appears they did not "boost" the US economy, but rather played a role in the dotcom boom and bust that accelerated offshoring, primarily to–India. Do we want more of this?

Plus, in the midst of our 2009 banking crisis, it was reported that New York's financial area employed thousands of H-1Bs. [728] *Did H-1Bs create financial reports promoting offshoring our jobs? Do they expect us to believe we had a desperate shortage of accountants and analysts?*

"More of World's Talented Workers Opt to Leave USA", a 2009 *USA Today* article Wadhwa wrote said many were homesick and *wanted to return to their culture and families*. Others he surveyed who had worked in strategic high tech jobs were returning to China and India lured by *foreign government enticements*, better job opportunities, and the lower cost of living. [744]

What if over a million more H-1Bs get green cards, work here ten more years, and then return to their "home country"—where will that leave America? While if they leave now, we have enough unemployed high tech Americans to fill the jobs, ten years from now we will not be able to rebound. We need Americans with no divided loyalties whose *"home country"* is the United States to fill our medical and high tech jobs.

Rajat Gupta Found Guilty Insider Trading!

As mentioned earlier, outsourcing kingpin Rajat Gupta was found guilty of insider trading in 2012. The jury *"found Gupta guilty of leaking confidential information he learned as a Goldmans Sachs board member on September 23, 2008, and then phoning hedge-fund operator Raj Rajaratnam, who within a minute of getting the tip began buying $43 million in Goldman stock."* [1066] The prosecution had *"wire tap recordings of Hedgefund owner Raj Rajaratnam's cell phone."* Gupta was "charged with leaking details of *...market-moving events*." While the jury was sequestered, the judge commented, "It's not a case of one bad apple, but a bushel full." [1019] [1018]

Sri Lanka born Raj Rajaratnam had already been convicted in an earlier trial. [927] "Hedge Fund Manager Rajaratnam Guilty in Insider Trading Trial," a 2011, *USA Today* article told how he was fed information by *"middle-men at so-called expert network firms,"* through "a spider-web-like network of tipsters, including members of corporate boards, other hedge fund managers, former top executives at elite consulting firms and technology companies." Our government caught him on recordings *"making incriminating statements,"* that involved an estimated $63.8 million. [924]

What these trials were exposing was how "India's collectivist culture offers a ready foil to America's rampant individualism." Recall the 2005 article, *"The Indians are Coming—How Management Thinkers from India are Changing the Face of American Business."* It explained that they work as a collective not individually in their business dealings. [240]

Telephone tapping will only expose the tip of this shark's fin. The real teeth are the face to face deal making at <u>exclusive network meetings</u>. How can stock crimes by exclusive networks be investigated by prosecutors? The prime evidence may be to identify patterns of trading that demonstrate insider trading knowledge such as returns that far exceed other investors.

How many American families are homeless or cannot afford college because of stock fraud? *If immigrants commit such major crimes against Americans and our economy should they and their family lose their US citizenship?*

Mega Maze Insider Trading

A *nytimes.com* report in 2008, made an interesting observation: *"the housing boom, which like the technology stock bubble lured people in with seemingly instant and risk-free profits."* [682] Were the boom and bubble so similar because the same people were pulling the strings behind the scenes? 'Expert' networks that collaborate.

Ethnic networks with exclusive memberships can be used to create a privileged elite through what I will call *"mega maze insider trading."* The term "mega" is used because of the scale of insider information goes go way beyond just one company's stock. The term "maze" is used because the network's web makes it difficult to catch insider trading connections. The network supplies insider knowledge on multiple companies, plus it has people positioned who control the media, the timing and content of press releases and stock analysis. They have people who control venture capital and people who control buying, and more. Members who collaborate in secret have penetrated every nook of our society including our universities, businesses, banks, and government. They can create studies and feed deals to each other that scam an entire region like Silicon Valley, to even global deals.

To illustrate *"mega maze insider"* knowledge imagine if an exclusive network in Silicon Valley has members negotiating large outsourcing contracts for thousands of jobs with our high tech corporations. And, imagine they have people on both sides of the deals. They knew to buy stock in the outsourcing companies. Plus, bankers in the group know if they push home equity loans that the thousands of Americans losing their jobs will default and allow them to take Americans' homes well below market value. Others in the network could buy up US hotels and made a fortune renting to visa workers. They can spin off startups using technology secrets gathered by members with insider access to outsourcing clients design databases.

World Bank Funding India's Growth

The World Bank moved its back office work, previously done in the West, to developing countries in 2003. It outsourced software development, document management, and message communications to India's Satyam. [586] [776]

Subsequently, a *World Bank study in 2004 claimed that India was the ideal location for software companies.* The Bank planned to provide India $3 billion over a four year period. [124] It is interesting to note that Vinod Khosla's sister Meera Khosla worked at the World Bank. [188] She and Vinod were both working for organizations in charge of distributing massive amounts of money supplied by US sources to fund startups.

Time for a US Recovery

Note that India's prosperity came from "reshaping Corporate America!" Consider that since the dotcom crash in 2000, US companies that morphed into multinationals cut 2.9 million jobs in the US, and added 2.4 million jobs overseas. And that does not include the jobs US companies outsourced to foreign companies according to a *USA Today*, May 2011 report, "Why the Jobs are Going Over There." [923]

The 'transfer' of US technology, money, and jobs to foreign nations threatens the future of our country. It is time to put a stop to exploitation and protect our jobs, intellectual property, and financial institutions.

Chapter 22

Visa & Green Card Abuses

Jobs for US citizens should be our first priority.

While Congress didn't require companies to show that they tried to hire Americans first when they hired H-1Bs, *it did require employers to show they tried to hire Americans before they could sponsor H-1Bs for green cards.* [31] [35]

However, armies of lawyers got rich helping H-1Bs circumvent the law. *"Our Goal is clearly not to find a qualified and interested U.S. Worker,"* a lawyer was caught on video in 2007 saying. [666] If it has not been removed you can watch the video on YouTube: "*PERM Fake Job Ads defraud Americans to secure green cards.*") Lawyers were advising companies on how to avoid hiring Americans so they could get green cards!

Our Labor Department decided to audit green card applications in June 2008. The goal was to make sure that Americans got a chance at jobs they are qualified to fill. [709] The investigation centered on compliance with US law that *requires a company must first attempt to recruit and hire qualified American workers before sponsoring a foreign visa worker for a green card.* The jobs paid $80,000 yearly on average, and H-1Bs from India dominated the green card applications. The audit abruptly closed a few months later. What happened?

The ultimate irony is that H-1Bs took American's jobs by working well below the prevailing wage, but were trying to use attorneys to get green cards to lock the jobs in at about the same pay level as the Americans they displaced.

Proposed Green Cards for Foreign Students!

While the H-1Bs get "temporary" visas most apply for green cards that let them work in the US permanently. In 2007, there was such a big backlog of green card applicants, US Rep Zoe Lofgren (D-CA), had the audacity to introduce several bills that would allow foreign graduate students to get permanent residency green cards directly, instead of first getting H-1B visas. [731]

Obama appointments "Undermine American Workers"

Obama *"filled some of his top White House posts with people who not only support expanding the H-1B visa program, but also see offshore outsourcing as a plus for the U.S. economy,"* reported a 2009 article "H-1B, Offshoring Supporters Get Key Obama Administration Posts," in *ComputerWorld.* [730] Obama appointed Diana Farrell, *"former director of the McKinsey Global Institute."* to serve on the National Economic Council; and, Judd Greg, *who thought H-1Bs created US jobs,* to be Commerce Secretary.

Shockingly this article revealed: *"Indian offshore firms are the largest users of the H-1B visas and consider it critical to their delivery model for moving IT functions offshore. It is a point they have made repeatedly in U.S. Security and Exchange Commission filings."* [730] How can Congress allow this program to continue knowing it is used by India to take our high tech jobs?

Senator Chuck Grassley criticized Obama's appointees. And, Ron Hira, assistant professor at the Rochester Institute of Technology, said Obama, *"is either ignorant or naïve about the real job market for American IT workers. He is doing his level best, with these appointments, to undermine American workers and their livelihoods."* [730]

Obama said: *"We should allow immigrants who earn their degrees in the U.S. to stay, work and become Americans over time. And we should examine our ability to increase the number of permanent visas we issue to foreign-skilled workers."* [731] So, Obama harmed young American college students who trusted and supported him. We need to stop this abuse.

Obama's Plan to Grant Millions of Green Cards

While Americans were suffering from high unemployment, Obama was trying to grant millions of green cards to foreign workers–which *are only supposed to be granted when no Americans can fill the jobs.*

"Easier Route to Green Card to be Proposed for Some," this *New York Times* story, told how <u>Obama was frustrated because his efforts to grant "*legal status to **millions of illegal immigrants**"* was being blocked by Congress, so he was looking for a way to bypass "dissention in Congress."</u> [978]

India and China had huge backlogs of H-1B green card applicants, and were lobbying intensely to end our 7% per country limit on green cards.

To learn more, read the book <u>Democracy Hijacked</u>. For example:

- ■ *"On November 29, 2011, the House passed a bill HR 3012 to repeal per country limits on green cards for visa workers. This legislation was sponsored by Jason Chaffetz (R, UT), and cosponsored by 5 Republicans: Jeff Flake (AZ), Robert Goodlatte (VA), Tim Griffin (AR) Lamar Smith (TX), Glenn Thompson (PA): and by 6 Democrats: Luis Gutierrez (IL), Rush Holt (NJ), Jesse Jackson Jr. (IL), Zoe Lofgren (CA), Carolyn Maloney (NY), James Moran Jr. (VA)." [974]*

- ■ *In January 2012, this bill granting millions of green cards still had to pass the Senate. It was being held by Senator Grassley who was standing up for American workers. You should let Grassley know how much you appreciate his efforts, and let your senators know if you oppose this bill.*

Each work-based Green Card is a job loss for an American.

Chapter 23

It is Time for the Sleeping Giant

to Wakeup

"Liberty cannot be preserved without a general knowledge among the people, who have a right ... and a desire to know ..." —*John Adams*

The purpose of this book is to help get America back on track economically by providing an economic recovery model—the Economic Circulation Model™. This model shows that it is essential to get Americans back to work and stop the transfer of our jobs to foreign workers.

We started this journey in search of our 15 million lost jobs. The dotcom crash in 2000, and the financial crisis in 2008, caused massive jobs losses, yet unlike previous recessions most of the Americans who lost their jobs never got their jobs back.

Recall from Chapter 1 that Jim Tankersley observed: *"America's jobs crisis began a decade ago. Long before the housing burst and Wall Street melted down."* He noted that: *"Before we can fix our jobs machine, we must first figure out what broke it."* [972]

Economics professors in our top universities were puzzled. They could not understand *"our lost decade of job growth."* –*"It's the trillion-dollar question....something big has happened. I really don't think we have a complete story yet."* *"Researchers are just starting to piece together the evidence, and no one can yet finger the culprit."*

He wanted to know why "*US job creation had stalled so spectacularly in the past decade?*"

- *We uncovered that the key was the H-1B fraud used by foreign workers to take our jobs and then to springboard our jobs to overseas workers.*

All the economists consulted said education was the key.

- *However, we discovered young Americans graduating from college were being denied jobs because of H-1Bs. Plus, that Americans who lost their jobs were well educated and highly skilled.*

He was puzzled over why US companies are setting on "*nearly $2 trillion in cash*" instead of investing it in "*domestic innovation and the jobs it should create.*" [972] And, labor economist Howard F. Rosen asked why US companies were investing overseas, instead of at home.

- *We uncovered that the number one reason US companies went overseas was incentives provided by foreign governments that lured our strategic high tech industries.* [615]

They asked why the US is losing our comparative advantage in college educated brain power.

- *We learned about student visa fraud, and how our universities have been co-opted to educate our foreign competition. There has been a foreign takeover some of our high tech graduate school programs.*

Why our population grew faster than our workforce?

- *Non-immigrant student and work visas were used illegally for mass immigration to the US.*

Tankersley asked. Should we invest more?

- *No. We should spend less, and invest more wisely. We should stop funding research done by foreign workers and foreign nations.*

Should we cut back on foreign trade?

- *Importing foreign visa workers is not trade, nor is outsourcing our jobs to foreign nations –it is dispossession.*

How to "Fix Our Jobs Machine"

Steps we need to take to fix our broken "Jobs Machine."

1. As mentioned earlier Wadhwa said there were over 1 million pending green card applications. And recall that sponsors are required to try to hire Americans first. Instead of green cards, the right thing to do is to post the jobs and put 1 million unemployed Americans back to work. Plug this into the Economic Circulation Model, $163,000 times one million jobs equals a *boost of $163 billion annually to our economy*.

2. It is time to offer incentives for businesses to hire Americans. If there are currently 5 million "temporary" (H-1B, L1,...) visa workers in the US, and employers replace them with Americans that would be $163,000 times 5 million *a boost of $815 billion per year to our economy*.

3. If we also end offshore tax incentives and 10 million jobs are brought back to the United States *$205,000 times 10 million a boost of $2.05 trillion per year*.

4. *End all tax subsidies for employing foreign workers*. It is not right to tax Americans to subsidize hiring foreigners taking their jobs. H-1B fees should be set at $160,000 each per year not $6,000. Plus *employers, not taxpayers, should cover costs such as educating foreign workers' children*.

5. Require that Americans be hired to fill tax funded jobs such as jobs in our universities, government, and government contractors.

6. Fill our colleges and graduate schools doing research with American students. The *quality of instruction needs to improve and the costs need to dramatically decrease*. If research jobs and other campus jobs hire Americans then young Americans should owe little, if any, college loan debt when they graduate.

7. The root of our job losses traces to our government's granting excessive foreign student visas, and failure to enforce immigration laws. We need to cut back from over 700,000 foreign student visas to around 10,000 or less per year. These 10,000 should pass careful background screening and be outstanding scholars who want to become loyal Americans. *If they excel in their studies they should get automatic green cards.*

8. We may also want to educate 1,000 per year of foreign student ambassadors in one year curriculum studies structured to create mutually beneficial ambassadors to foreign nations. Ambassadors would not be eligible for visa extensions, work visas nor green cards.

9. Stop using our taxes to fund business development in foreign nations.

10. Pass laws that prohibit foreign outsourcing companies from operating in the US. The prime business model of these companies is displacing American workers with foreign workers.

11. Revoke the H-1B visa and similar programs that were abused to displace American workers. Most H-1Bs are employed by our federal and state government agencies, US businesses, and US universities.

12. Employ Americans, not foreigners to do sensitive government research in *biology, computer science, engineering, nanotechnology, biological warfare defense, space programs, network-centric warfare technology, guidance technology, and much more..* We spend billions through The National Science Foundation (NSF), The Defense Advanced Research Project Agency, The National Institute of Standards and Technology (NIST), and more. [515]

Avoiding Pitfalls & Prejudice

It is important to note that Americans loyal to America come from many races. While the ethnic networks involved in H-1B visa fraud and outsourcing and stock market manipulations are predominantly Asian, it is important to remember that the American executives and politicians involved are predominantly white. Moreover, these executives in some cases were also responsible for exploiting workers in Asia. Key partners in sorting out this mess may well be Americans of Asian ancestry who love our country and who have no connections to the ethnic networks.

While we help fellow Americans recover, we need to minimize the harm to people in China and India, the majority of whom had nothing to do with these harmful visa programs and outsourcing. The people involved in these ethnic networks probably make up less than 1% of the population in China and in India. Moreover, it is not in the best interest of the majority of people in China or India for the US to collapse. Nor is it in our best interests that they be harmed.

Beware the 99% Nonsense

We need to tread very carefully. If someone became a millionaire because they came up with an invention or business worth millions then they earned the money. Redistribution of wealth that people earned goes against the American way. Some people are more talented or work harder than others so it is fair for them to earn more money. Wealth redistribution is bad if it rewards lazy people or acts as a disincentive to build businesses.

However, if a millionaire got rich through displacing Americans with foreign workers, or stock manipulations or other unscrupulous means that's a different story. They did not earn the money. In this case some means of wealth distribution back to the victims is the right thing to do. Especially, if such redistribution can be used to get people back to work and stimulate our economy.

We Need Creative Solutions for Economic Recovery

If we work together we can restore our economy, reclaim our jobs and build a better future for our children.

Each generation faces its own struggles to preserve freedom and prosperity. The future of America is in our hands. There is much that needs to be done.

Bibliography

Referenced sources are arranged in numeric order according to the reference numbers located in [brackets] in the document text. This book is the culmination of extensive research; only sources referenced in this book are included in this bibliography. Therefore, you will see breaks in the number sequence such as: reference number "6" followed by reference number "8", because reference number "7" in the complete documents list was not used in this book.

Note: Web addresses do not include the www prefix, and only contain the first part of the path. This address information or a search engine query for the title should be sufficient to help locate the articles and websites. Note also that some articles may have been removed, and some websites may have been changed from the time the research was done.

1: Rupert Cornwell, *Interview: Professor JK Galbraith*, The Independent, 1-Jul-02.

2: Holly Sklar, *Up, Up and Away: CEO Compensation*, www.inequality.org, 2000.

3: David Batstone, *CEO Compensation Keeps Rising*, www.worthwhilemag.com, 29-May-04.

4: Ed Frauenheim, *For CEOs, Offshoring Pays*, builder.com.com, 1-Sep-04.

5: Studies, *New CEO/Worker Pay Gap Study*, Institute for Policy Studies and United for a Fair Economy, 2001.

6: Sarah Anderson, John Cavanagh, Chris Hartman, Scott Klinger, and Stacy Chan, *Executive Excess 2004 Campaign Contributions, Outsourcing, Unexpensed Stock Options and Rising CEO Pay*, Institute for Policy Studies and United for a Fair Economy, 31-Aug-04.

8: Bruce Nussbaum, *Can You Trust Anybody Anymore?*, Business Week online, 28-Jan-02.

9: Geoffrey Colvin, *Executive Pay The Great CEO Pay Heist*, www.fortune.com, Web Date 1/23/2004.

11: Kurt Eichenwald, *Big Paychecks are Exhibit A at C.E.O. Trials*, The New York Times, 19-Jun-05.

12: Associated Press, *Senate Votes to Add More Visas for Foreign Workers*, Dallas Morning News, 19-May-98.

13: Jeri Clausing, *Senate Passes Bill Increasing Foreign Worker Visas*, New York Times, 19-May-98.

14: Jim Puzzanghera, *Senate Votes to Boost High-Tech Visas*, San Jose Mercury News, 18-May-98.

15: Louis Freedberg, *Senate Oks High-Tech Worker Bill*, San Francisco Chronicle, 19-May-98.

21: Robert R. Prechter Jr., *Conquer the Crash*, John Wiley & Sons, LTD, Hoboken, New Jersey, 2002.

22: *Highly Charged Visa Bill*, opensecrets.org, 3-Aug-98, Web Date 1/30/2002.

24: Dr. Norman Matloff, *Debunking the Myth of a Desperate Software Labor Shortage*, heather.cs.ucdavis.edu, 8-Jul-01.

26: Dr. Norman Matloff, *Modern Day Slaves*, netslaves.com, 30-Dec-00.

27: Gary Cohn and Walter F. Roche Jr., *How Many Visas? Uh, we don't know*, Sunspot/zazona.com, 21-Feb-00.

28: Rescue American Jobs, *Amazing Facts and Statistics: Non-Immigrant (Temporary) Foreign Work Visa Programs and Workers*, rescueamericanjobs.org, Web Date 5/26/2005.

29: Rep. Tom Tancredo, *H-1B Visas -- A Time to Cut Back*, h1bprotest.com, 30-Dec-02.

30: Pradipta Bagchi, *Visas for business or bondage?*, y-axix.com, 6-Jul-00.

31: Kim Berry, *Does the U.S. still need H-1B programmers?*, prestwood.com, Web Date 11/1/2002.

32: *H-1B visa: Your trip may be harrowing*, The Times of India, 11-Apr-01.

33: U.S. Border Control, *High Tech Worker Tells His Story*, usbc.org, 7-Mar-98.

34: AFL CIO, *H-1B Fact Sheet Why S. 2045 Should be Defeated*, dpeaflcio.org, 2001, Web Date 7/20/2005.

35: Jeff Nachtigal, *Can You Find a Job for my Friend?*, washtech.org, 7-Oct-02.

36: Chris Currie, *IEEE-USA/Harris Poll: U.S. Public Overwhelmingly Opposed to H-1B Visa Expansion*, ieeeusa.org, 16-Sep-98.

37: Programmers Guild, *How to Underpay H-1B Workers*, programmersguild.org, Web Date 7/20/2005.

40: Associated Press, *H-1B Visa Demand Rises*, asianweek.com, 7-Feb-02.

41: INS, *Characteristics of Specialty Occupation Workers (H-1B)*, U.S. Immigration and Naturalization Service, 1-Feb-00.

42: Rachel Konrad, Staff Writer, *H-1B Visas Jump in 2001*, news.com.com, 22-Jan-02.

43: Rob Sanchez, *H-1B Newsletter Get the Facts on H-1B*, zazona.com, 28-Jun-02.

44: Ed Frauenheim, *Scourge of Silicon Valley --4*, salon.com, 19-Oct-00.

45: Ed Frauenheim, *Scourge of Silicon Valley --5*, salon.com, 19-Oct-00.

46: Linda Kilcrease, *Problems with the H-1B Expansion and T-Visas*, zazona.com, 4-May-01.

47: Dr. Gene A. Nelson, *A Brief History of H-1B*, zazona.com, 4-May-01.

49: Kevin Hattori, CNN Reporter, *Economy and Job Market in Silicon Valley*, ieeeusa.org, 14-Sep-02.

51: Barbara Rose, Chicago Tribune, *Tech Veterans Squeezed Out: Overseas Hiring, Ageism Blamed*, seattletimes.nwsource.com, 14-Mar-02.

54: Tech Law Journal, *Senate Holds Hearings on H-1B Visas*, techlawjournal.com, 25-Feb-98.

55: Martin Desmarais, *Lawsuit Slams Sun's 'Bias' for Indian H-1B Workers*, indusbusinessjournal.com, 1-Apr-03.

56: Rachel Konrad staff writer, *'Body Shop' must pay fees in H-1B Lawsuit*, news.com.com, 25-Apr-01.

58: Peter Brimelow, *New H-1B Scandal - Tax Evasion!*, vdare.com, 24-Sep-00.

59: *Demographics of the Typical H-1B*, zazona.com, Web Date 4/24/2001.

60: *A Legislative History of H-1B and Other Immigrant Work Visas*, zazona.com, Web Date 8/11/2004.

62: Margaret Quan, *IEEE USA Presses Congress on Visa Curbs*, theworkcircuit.com, 26-Mar-03.

63: Phyllis Schlafly Report, *What the Global Economy Costs Americans*, eagleforum.org, 3-Jun-03.

65: Dr. Norman Matloff, *ITAA Opposes Giving Americans Hiring Priority*, engology.com, 27-Jan-05.

66: Greg Levine, *Welch: GE Ex-CEO Blasts Outsourcing Opponents*, forbes.com, 11-May-04.

67: Winston Chai, CNETAsia, *India: IT Outsourcing Aids U.S. Other Economies*, asia.cnet.com, 14-Jul-03.

68: David M. Halbfinger, *Outsourcing Kerry Urges Voters to Look Past Bush's 'Last-Minute Promises'*, New York Times, 4-Sep-04.

69: Dean Baker and David Rosnick, *Bad Sources on "Insourcing"*, cepr.net, 24-Mar-04.

71: *American IT Pros Sue, Bangalore Shivers*, timesofindia.indiatimes.com, 22-Mar-04.

72: Rachel Konrad, AP Staff Writer, *Outsourcing Backlash Brewing*, cbsnews.com, 19-Jan-04.

73: *Hard Times in Silicon Valley*, cbsnews.com, 14-Jul-03.

74: *Hire American Citizens*, hireamericancitizens.org, 11-Jun-03.

80: RTTS Services - Outsourcing Statistics, *Statistic Related to Offshore Outsourcing*, rttsweb.com, 27-May-05.

81: Paul Craig Roberts, *Outsourcing: A Greater Threat Than Terrorism*, newsmax.com, 22-Apr-05.

83: Andy McCue, *Gartner: Outsourcing Costs more than in-house*, news.com.com, 4-Mar-05.

84: Ed Frauenheim, Staff Writer, CNET News.com, *Study: Software makers head offshore*, news.com.com, 21-Jul-03.

86: Chidanand Rajghatta, *US gives India Assurance on Outsourcing*, Economic Times of India, 14-Jun-03.

88: Board of Directors, *IEEE USA: Position Offshore Outsourcing*, ieeeusa.org, 1-Mar-04.

90: *Outsourcing to India*, gnp.org/india, Web Date 3/31/2003.

91: Todd Jatras, *Can India Retain Its Reign As Outsourcing King?*, forbes.com, 28-Feb-01.

95: The Economic Times Online, *US IT Biggies Recalling BPO jobs*, economictimes.indiatimes.com, 28-Apr-04.

96: Abhay Vaidya, *H-1B Cap No Big Issue for IT Firms*, economictimes.indiatimes.com, 31-Oct-03.

98: The Economic Times Online, *India BPO guy: Hero or Villain?*, economictimes.indiatimes.com, 28-Apr-04.

100: David Zielenziger, Reuters, *Corrected - US Companies Quietly Moving More Jobs Overseas*, money.excite.com, 24-Dec-03.

102: Ed Frauenheim, Staff Writer, CNET News, *U.S. Firms Move IT Overseas*, news.com.com, 11-Dec-02.

105: Jennifer Bjorhus, San Joes Mercury News, *USA: Slowdown Sending Tech Jobs Overseas*, corpwatch.org, 21-Oct-02.

108: Business News, *Documents' Honeywell plans to add 5,500 aerospace jobs overseas*, start.earthlink.net, 7-Dec-04.

113: Ed Frauenheim, *Coding: Should it Stay or Should it Go?*, CNET News.com, 22-Jul-03.

117: The Hindu Business Line, *Sun Grows 70 pc, Expands India Presence*, blonnet.com, 29-Jun-00.

118: Express Computer India, *Sun Microsystems India turns up the heat on competition*, expresscomputeronline.com, 24-Dec-01.

119: *India to See R&D Outsourcing Boom*, rediff.com, 26-Apr-04.

121: Rashmi Sharma Singh, *H Workers in Limbo*, indolink.com, 30-Jan-01.

122: Terry Atlas, *Bangalore's Big Dreams*, U.S. News & World Report, 2-May-05.

123: K.C. Krishnadas, *India's Tech Industry Defends H-1B, Outsource Roles*, Electronic Engineering Times.com, 10-Jul-03.

124: India Business Opportunities, *Electronics & Information Technology*, ficci.com/ficci/india-profile, Web Date 11/4/2002.

125: United Press International, *High-tech Industry Fires Americans, Hires Indians*, newsmax.com, 20-Mar-03.

126: Associated Press, *Dell to Stop Using Tech Support in India*, earthlink.net, 24-Nov-03.

128: *Regional Advantage Notes - ITEC 1210 (IT Revolution)*, greenvertigo.net, 1-Nov-01.

129: Ron Schneiderman, *Outsourcing: How Safe is Your Job?*, Electronic Design, 10-May-04.

132: Geoffrey James, *How Companies Court Disaster in Outsourcing Deals*, computerworld.com, 30-Oct-00.

134: The Economic Times Online, *India Jobs Offer Tax-Breaks to US, Inc.*, economictimes.indiatimes.com, 6-Apr-04.

135: Christopher H. Schmitt, *Wages of Sin - Why Lawbreakers still win government contracts*, U.S. News & World Report, 13-May-02.

137: Washington Technology, *Top 100*, Washingtontechnology.com, 7-May-01.

140: Jamie Horwitz, *White -Collar Meltdown*, dpeaflcio.org, 4-Jun-04.

141: *Shipping Jobs Overseas: How Real is the Problem*, aflcio.org, Web Date 5/27/2005.

142: David Cay Johnston, *Americans' Income Shrank for 2 Consecutive Years?*, dailyreckoning.com, Web Date 8/23/2004.

143: Rescue American Jobs, *American Jobs for Americans First - Amazing Facts*, rescueamericanjobs.org, Web Date 9/23/2003.

144: Rep Tom Tancredo Congressional Testimony, *Enforcing Immigration Laws Would Create 10 Million Jobs!*, rescueamericanjobs.org, 18-Jun-03.

153: *Here is a list of Some of the Largest India Owned Bodyshops*, zazona.com, Web Date 9/6/2004.

154: Edwin S. Rubenstein, *Can Immigrants Save Social Security?*, zazona.com, 5-Dec-03.

156: Citizens for Tax Justice, *Surge in Corporate Tax Welfare Drives Corporate Tax Payments to Near Record Low*, ctj.org, 17-Apr-02.

161: Embassy of India, *India's Information Technology Industry*, indianembassy.org, Web Date 5/27/2005.

170: Albert H. Teich, *R&D in the Federal Budget: Frequently Asked Questions*, aaas.org, Web Date 8/23/2005.

175: Gretchen Hyman, *India, the Jewel in Oracle's Crown*, siliconvalley.internet.com, 31-Jul-02.

176: U.S. Commercial Service India, *Computer and Software Services*, buyusa.gov, 6-Nov-02.

186: Dr. Norman Matloff, *H-1B/L-1/Offshoring e-Newsletter*, engology.com, 4-Apr-05.

187: Anthony Spaeth/New Delhi, *Golden Diaspora*, indianembassy.org, 7-Mar-01.

188: Wikipedia, *Vinod Khosla*, wikipedia.org, Web Date 8/15/2005.

189: The Hindu, *3 Indians on Forbes Midas List*, hinduonnet.com/thehindu, 15-Feb-05.

190: Desi Flavor, *Plugging India's Brain Drain*, jgohil.typepad.com/desiflavor, 2-Jun-04.

191: A P Kamath in Chicago, *TiE Company Forum to Discuss Biz Strategies, Models*, rediff.com, 20-Sep-99.

192: *Interesting facts about India and Indians!*, hindustanlink.com, 2000.

197: Leon E Panetta, *Lessons Not Learned: California's $35 Billion in Red Ink Calls for Fearless Leaders*, panettainstitue.org, 12-Jan-03.

205: Eric Chabrow, *IT Innovation Drives Homeland-Security Efforts*, informationweek.com, 25-Feb-02.

220: Michael Singer, *DOD Taps Verity for Military Intelligence*, siliconvalley.internet.com, 23-Jul-02.

221: *U.S. Leads Science and Engineering but for How Much Longer*, Machine Design, 7-Oct-04.

224: Hearing of the Immigration and Claims Subcommittee, *Oral Testimony of Gene A,. Nelson, Ph.D. Regarding U.S. High Tech Workforce*, zazona.com, 5-Aug-99.

226: David Kirkpatrick, Fortune.com, *Will the U.S. Fall Behind in Tech?*, cnn.com, 23-Oct-02.

228: Ashank Desai, *Making of a Software Superpower*, timescomputing.com, 31-Mar-99.

229: Jim Montague and Mark Hoske, *Calmer Waters?*, Control Engineering, 1-May-03.

230: George J. Borjas, National Review, *Rethinking Foreign Students: A Question of National Interest*, ksghome.harvard.edu, 17-Jun-02.

235: Kellogg School of Management, *Academics & Faculty, Mohanbir Sawhney*, www1.kellog.northwestern.edu, 1-Jul-05.

236: *How Divine was this Venture?*, siliconindia.com, 2-Jan-01.

237: David Whitford, *Press Coverage, The Intellectual Capitalist*, splitthedifference.com, 17-Apr-00.

238: Marc Ballon, Los Angeles Times, *Professors Profiting from Practicing What They Teach*, kellogg.northwestern.edu, 16-Jul-00.

239: Mohanbir Sawhney, *Getting to Global*, Profiting from Transparency, 2-Oct-03.

240: Des Dearlove and Stuart Crainer, The Conference Board, *The Indians Are Coming, How Management Thinkers From India are Changing the Face of American Business*, conference-board.org, 1-Jul-05.

242: About Us, *Editorial Board of siliconindia*, siliconindia.com, 2000.

244: Chidanand Rajghatta, *Wireless Whisper: Design Network Begins to Takeover Telecom World*, indianexpress.com, 13-Jul-00.

245: The Economic Times Online, *US Professors: New Age Ambassadors of India Inc.*, economictimes.indiatimes.com, 8-Apr-04.

246: Michael Dorgan, *Chinese Families Pay Big Money for U.S. Student Visas*, americanvisas.com, 2-Apr-00.

250: Tom Biggs, Senior Hardware Engineer, Hammerhead Systems, *Don't Blame Students for Declining EE Grad Numbers*, Electronic Engineering Times, 14-Mar-05.

252: Federation for American Immigration Reform, *Foreign Students in the United States*, fairus.org, 4-Nov-04.

253: Tom Walsh, *University of Michigan Center in India Aims to Help U.S.*, thebatt.com, 19-May-04.

254: George Borjas, *An Evaluation of the Foreign Student Program*, cis.org, 1-Jun-02.

255: Paul Craig Roberts, *War, Outsourcing and Debt. Delusion Rules*, axisoflogic.com, 30-Sep-04.

256: Chidanand Rajghatta, *Brain Curry: American Campuses Crave for IIT of Glory*, indian-express.com, 7-Dec-00.

261: Associated Press, *U.S. Flunks Higher Education Affordability*, earthlink.net, 15-Sep-04.

262: Leslie D'Monte, *MIT Media Lab in India*, zdnetindia.com, 15-Feb-01.

263: College Savings Bank, *College Costs*, collegesavings.com, Web Date 1/12/2003.

264: June Kronholz, *Who Can Fix Higher (Cost) Education*, The Wall Street Journal, 1-Aug-04.

267: Joseph Farah, *The Prince and The Media*, wnd.com, 7-Nov-01.

271: The Daily Reckoning, *Rude Awakening*, dailyreckoning.com, 27-May-05.

272: Numbers USA, *Did Congress Intend a huge Increase in Numbers after 1965?*, numbersusa.com/overpopulation, Web Date 2/27/2005.

281: *Washington Largest Gathering of Indian Americans at State Banquet*, evishwagujarati.net, 1-Nov-00.

286: David M Boje, *Enron is Theatre*, cbae.nmsu.edu, 21-Sep-02.

288: Sanjeev Srivastava in Bombay, *India's High-Tech Hopes*, bbc.co.us, 17-Mar-00.

289: Melanie Warner, *The Indians of Silicon Valley*, Fortune, 15-May-00.

292: *Investment Scams: Pump and Dump*, investopedia.com, Web Date 7/13/2005.

293: Dvorak, *Dot Conned and The American Way*, dvorak.org, 8-Mar-05.

294: Stock Market Crash!, *The Nasdaq Bubble*, stock-market-crash.net, Web Date 7/13/2005.

295: *The Dot-Com Crash: March 11, 2000 to October 9, 2002*, investopedia.com, Web Date 7/13/2005.

296: Alan Stewart and Paul McLaughlin, CA Magazine, *The Dirt on the Dot.Cons*, kkc.net, 1-Jul-01.

297: Associated Press --Curt Anderson contributed, *Ex-Computer Associates CEO Kumar Indicted*, earthlink.net, 23-Sep-04.

298: Robert L Grant, Dow Jones Newswires, *Lay, Other Enron Directors' Seats on Boards Face Scrutiny*, quicken.com, 25-Jan-02.

299: Rob Spiegel, *Dot Com Crash: Whose Fault is it Anyway?*, theezine.net, 8-Dec-01.

300: Manjeet Kripalani and Pete Engardio, *The Rise of India*, BusinessWeek, 8-Dec-03.

301: Mike Yamamoto, staff writer Cnet News.com, *Will India Price Itself out of the Offshore Market?*, freeborders.com, 29-Mar-04.

302: Richard Armstrong, *H-1B Myth: The Best and the Brightest*, americanreformation.org, Web Date 12/4/2002.

303: Manjeet Kripalani in Bombay, with Pete Engardia and Leah Nathans Spiro in New York, *India's WHIZ KIDS (int'l edition), Inside the Indian Institutes of Technology's Star Factory*, businessweek.com/1998/49/b3607011.htm, 25-Nov-98.

304: IndiaExpress Bureau, *Those Magnificent Indians in Forbes List*, indiaexpress.com, 23-Sep-00.

305: The Red Herring Magazine, *The Bucks Start Here: The Leading Venture Capital Firms of 1996*, Frontenac Company, 1-Jun-97.

306: *Investor Entrepreneur Forum at siliconindia Annual Conference 2001*, siliconindia.com, 2000.

308: CBS Worldwide Inc., *Out of India*, cbsnews.com, 11-Jan-04.

309: Ela Dutt, *7 Indian Americans Among 'Forbes' 400 Richest*, timesofindia.com, 24-Sep-00.

310: *TiE-Rockies Speakers 2000-2001*, tie-rockies.org, Web Date 5/14/2002.

312: Alex Salkever, The Industry Standard, *The Curry Network*, tie-carolinas.org, 24-Jan-00.

315: Special Correspondent, *IIT Alumni Gesture to the Alma Mater*, the-hindu.com, 9-Dec-99.

319: Raja Bose, Times News Network, *NRI Hunts for Talent in India*, indiaday.org, 19-Nov-03.

320: Hindustantimes.co, Press Trust of India, *Eighteen Indian Companies in Forbes' List*, indiaday.org, 5-Nov-03.

323: Lesly Stahl, *Imported from India*, 60 Minutes, 2-Mar-03.

324: *Rebuttal from Norm Matloff*, hireamericancitizens.org, 1-Jul-03.

327: Dr. Norman Matloff, *Bias at CBS*, itaa.org, 21-Sep-03.

329: Dr. Norman Matloff, *Needed Reform for the H-1B Work Visa: Major Points*, heather.cs.ucdavis.edu, 7-May-03.

330: Chidanand Rajghatta, *Where Integrated Chip means Indians, Chinese*, indian-express.com, 23-Feb-00.

331: Kevin Wu, New York City, *The Silicon Valley Indians*, bebeyond.com, 2002.

332: *Organizational Profile: The IndUS Entrepreneurs (TiE)*, larta.org, 14-Jun-01.

333: Vanessa Richardson, *The 'Indian Mafia' Muscles onto the Web*, redherring.com, 14-Dec-99.

334: Vishwas Varghese, *Information Superpower India?*, swordoftruth.com, 20-May-00.

335: Y--Axis: Recruit from India, *The Indian Software Industry*, y-axis.com, Web Date 11/4/2002.

338: Sreeni Meka's Immigration Issues, *Who Uses High-Skill Visas*, angelfire.co, Web Date 11/4/2002.

341: Melanie Warner, Fortune, *Could Telecom be Carlyle's New Defense*, openflows.org, 18-Mar-02.

344: Spencer E. Ante, New York, *The Secret Behind Those Profit Jumps*, BusinessWeek, 8-Dec-03.

345: *TiE-NY -- Membership*, spidersweb.com/tie, Web Date 10/6/2005.

347: Viji Sundaram, India-West Staff Reported, *India West: Kanwal Rekhi Joins ISN Advisory Board*, isn.org, 4-May-01.

348: Murali Krishna Devarakonda, *Kanwal Rekhi advises Laid-off H-1B workers not to Leave*, isn.org, 29-Apr-01.

349: *Kanwal Rekhi School of Information Technology*, it.iitb.ac.in, Web Date 9/27/2005.

350: Emeral Yeh, *Kanwal Rekhi Biography 2001*, asianpacificfund.org, Web Date 9/27/2005.

351: David Mildenberg, *Networking Godfather to Visit Triangle*, bizjournals.com, 25-Sep-00.

354: Sean Gregory, *Rainmaking 101*, Time Bonus Section, 1-Nov-04.

355: William K Tabb, *New Economy ?Same Irrational Economy*, monthlyreview.org, 2-Apr-01.

357: Kamla Bhatt, *From Meerut to Silicon Valley: The $11-billion Story*, rediff.com, 3-May-00.

358: IANS san Jose, *Dotcom Shakeout has Set Things Right'*, hindustantimes.com, 11-Dec-00.

359: Ajay Singh, *Upstarts How India's dotcom Pioneers Staked their Claims in Silicon Valley Your Space*, asiaweek.com, 23-Nov-01.

360: Pallava Bagla, *Indian Schools Cash In on Silicon Valley Wealth*, wbln0018.worldbank.org, 11-May-00.

361: Priya Ganapati, *Giving Back to the Alma Mater, IIT Alumni Style*, iitbombay.org, 1-Feb-02.

362: Associated Press, *Tech Downturn Doesn't Slow H-1B Visas*, apnew.excite.com, 28-Jan-02.

363: Brian Sullivan, *Emotions Run Hot on H-1Bs*, computerworld.com, 29-Apr-02.

364: Thomas W. Hazlett, Special to ZDNet, *Why Are We in a Broadband Recession?*, excite.com, 30-Jul-01.

365: Robert Thompson, LookSmart, *Scrutinizing the Scrutineers: How accurate are high technology's pithy pundits?*, findarticles.com, 1-Sep-98.

366: Namita Bhandare, Dew Delhi, *Indian CEOs Still Riding High in US Despite Two Exits*, hindustantimes.com, 12-Apr-01.

367: Non-Resident Indians, *Forbes 500 Honors Indian Entrepreneurs*, welcome-nri.com, 1-Jan-00.

369: *The Greedy Bunch*, fortune.com, 2-Sep-02.

371: Penelope Patsuris, *Forbes Dropoffs*, forbes.com, 22-Jun-01.

372: AnnaLee Saxenian, *Silicon Valley's New Immigrant Entrepreneurs*, The Center for Comparative Immigration Studies, University of California, San Diego, 1-May-00.

373: Denver Business Journal, *Qwest lawsuits Settled*, bizjournals.com, 18-Feb-04.

377: Anonymous, *I am Proud to be a Indian are You?*, geocities.com, Web Date 11/4/2002.

378: Shyamanuja Das and Ch Srinivas Rao, *Tech Start-ups: Indus Valley, Circa 2002*, CIOL Cybertimes, voicendata.com, 7-Sep-02.

379: NPR-- All Things Considered, Outsourcing entrepreneurs going back home to export American jobs, *neoIT-Atul Vashistha Discusses Outsourcing*, neoit.com, 16-Mar-04.

387: CNN Tonight, *Harvey Pitt Announced SEC will bring in McKinsey Mgt Consulting to perform a Top to Bottom Analyis of SEC Operations*, h1bvisasucks.com, 18-Jul-02.

388: Broc Romanek, *270-Page Report on SEC's Weaknesses*, thecorporatecounsel.net, 1-Dec-03.

389: Organizations and Scofflaws that Shill H-1B, *Public Policy Institute of California (PPIC)*, zazona.com, Web Date 10/17/2005.

390: INDOlink-International and NRI News, *Silicon Spice Acquired by Broadcom for $1.2 Billion*, indolink.com, 7-Aug-00.

395: *Despite Tech Crash, Premji Remains Richest Indian*, newsindia-times.com, 29-Jun-01.

397: Philip Martin and Peter Duigan, *Recent Immigration Patterns*, Hoover Press, 2003.

400: Y-Axis The H-1B Co., *Statistics and Trivia*, y-axis.com, Web Date 9/26/2005.

421: Financial News, *i2 Settles Class Action and Derivative Lawsuits*, biz.yahoo.com/bw/040510/105480 1.html, 10-May-04.

431: Janet Kornblum and Alex Lash, *Pockets Run Deep for Java*, news.cnet.com, 20-Aug-96.

432: Jill Steinberg, *Java Gets $100 Million Endorsement*, javaworld.com, 1-Sep-96.

440: Project on Government Oversight, *Government Contractors Wield Influence Through Revolving Door, Campaign Contributions*, pogo.org, 29-Jun-04.

451: Wayne Labs, Contributing Editor, *The Shifting Design Cycle*, Electron Design, 20-Oct-05.

455: M.R. Rangaswami, Co-founder, Sand Hill Group LLC, *The Next Wave of Software Business Strategy*, sterlinghoffman.com/newsletter/articles/article 103.html, Web Date 11/5/2005.

461: Richard B. Johnson, Project Engineer, Analogic Corp., Peabody, Mass, *I Created Jobs to Keep Americans Employed*, Electronic Engineering Times, 11-Jul-05.

462: David Roman, *Firms Grab Large Piece of Venture Pie*, Electronic Engineering Times, 30-Jan-06.

463: Ben Stocking, Mercury News, *The TiE That Binds*, slomedia.com/filles/press/20001127, 27-Nov-00.

464: Dr. Norman Matloff, H-1B/L-1/offshoring e-newsletter, *More on the CMU/TCS Connection*, heather.cs.ucdavis.edu, 25-Feb-04.

467: Arthur J Pais, *Jessie Jackson is Blowing Smoke,' Says TiE's Rekhi*, rediff.com, 4-Jun-99.

468: Gary Cohn and Walter Fl. Roche, Baltimore Sun, *Indentured Servants for High-Tech Trade Labor*, ailf.org/pubed/n022100a.htm, 21-Feb-00.

469: The Official Website of the Department of IT and Biotechnology, Government of Karnataka, *TiE Con - Speakers Profile*, bangaloreit.com/html/itscbng/tieconspeak.htm, 2000.

477: Anthony Kujawa, Washington File Staff Writer, *Foreign Student Enrollment at U.S. Graduate Schools Up in 2005*, usinfo.state.gov, 7-Nov-05.

478: Wikipedia, *James Gosling*, http://en.wikipedia.org/wiki/James Gosling, Web Date 12/21/2005.

479: Daniel Brook, *Are Your Lawyers in New York or New Delhi?*, legalaffairs.org, 1-Jun-05.

482: Wikipedia, *AnnaLee Saxenian*, http://en.wikipedia.org/wiki/AnnaLee Saxeian, 10-Dec-05.

484: Michael Fitzgerald, *Is U.S. Losing the Innovation Arms Race*, cioinsight.com, 5-Jun-05.

488: Edwin S. Rubenstein, The Hudson Institute, *Trade Drag?*, americanoutlook.org, 1-Jun-01.

491: Jim Turley, editor in chief of Embedded Systems Design, *Engineering Shortage? Get Real*, Electronic Engineering Times, 16-Jan-06.

492: Sadanand Dhume, *Hyderabad's Harvard: A University Built on an Arid Plain with Funds from Overseas Indians?*, fas.ulaval.ca/personnel/vernag/EH/F/cause/klectures/hyderabad harvard .htm, 8-Aug-02.

494: Dr. Norman Matloff, *Johnny Can So Program*, news.com.com, 10-May-05.

503: Jeffrey Pfeffer, *The Hidden Cost of Outsourcing*, cnnmoney.com, 1-Mar-06.

504: Paul Craig Roberts, *Nuking the Economy -- Forget Iran --Americans Should be Hysterical About This*, baltimorechronicle.com/2006, 13-Feb-06.

505: Jeannine Aversa, AP Economics Writer, *Bush Concedes Outsourcing Hurts Workers*, latimes.com/business/investing/wire/sns-ap-bush-outsourcing, 3-Mar-06.

510: DiamondCluster International, Inc, *2005 Global IT Outsourcing Study*, diamondcluster.com, 2005.

512: S.L. Bachman, Pacific Council on International Policy, The Western Partner of the Council on Foreign Relations, *Globalization in the San Francisco Bay Area: Trying to Stay at the Head of the Class*, , 2-Jan-03.

513: ABC News Internet Ventures, *A Billion Reasons to Care About India -- India is a Global Force to Be Reckoned With-- Its Economy is Booming*, abcnews.go.com/GMA, 1-Mar-06.

515: David Roman, *Bush's Budget, Up Close*, Electronic Engineering Times, 27-Feb-06.

516: IndiaTimes News Network, *Employee Files Class Action Suit Against Tata America*, economictimes.indiatimes.com, 15-Feb-06.

517: Wikipedia, *Spencer Abraham*, http://en.wikipedia.org/wiki/Spenser Abraham, Web Date 3/8/2006.

518: *Senator Spencer Abraham*, opensecrets.org, 31-Dec-00.

523: multiple authors, *Technology Without Borders Global iit2005 Conference*, iit2005.org, 2005.

528: Nicolas Mokhoff, *Have Engineers Come to Accept the Offshoring Phenomenon?*, Electronic Engineering Times, 21-Aug-06.

529: David Roman and Junko Yoshida, *State of the Engineer -- The Young and the Restless*, Electronic Engineering Times, 21-Aug-06.

531: Xinhua News Agency, *More Chinese Postgraduate Applicants Enrolled in US Universities*, china.org.cn, 21-Nov-06.

540: T.V. Mohandas Pai, Director and CFO, *The Infosys Financial Model*, infosys.com/investor/transcript/the infosysfinancial model.pdf, 2002.

549: Jim Whitehead, *Advice for Foreign Students Wishing to Pursue Graduate Study in Computer Science at UCSC*, cse.ucsc.edu, 8-Dec-05.

557: William Aspray, Frank Mayadas, Moshe Y. Vardi, Editors Association for Computing Machinery, *Job Migration Task Force*, acm.org/globalization report/summary, Web Date 3/11/2006.

558: *TechNet: Who We Are, Meetings with US Politicians, and Members*, technet.org, Web Date 3/22/2006.

559: Mother Jones, *John Doerr (with Ann), Donor Profile*, matherjones.com, 5-Mar-01.

565: Marcus Courtney, WashTech News, *Congress Considers Massive H-1B Visa Expansion, Gates Tells Congress It's Microsoft's Top Priority*, washtech.org/news/legislative, 21-Mar-06.

566: Michael A. Banak, PE, Crosstalk Town Hall, *Similar Fate Awaits H-1Bs Who Displaced American EEs*, Electronic Engineering Times, 12-Jun-06.

567: Sudhir Shah, Global Indian Takeover, *Worried About H-1B Visa? Take the L1 Route*, economictimes.indiatimes.com, 20-Mar-06.

568: Leslie Stahl, *North of the Border*, CBS News, "60 Minutes", 3-Oct-93.

576: Jordan Robertson, Associated Press, Miami Herald, *Engineer Indicted for Alleged Espionage*, herald.com, 14-Dec-06.

581: Associated Press, International Herald Tribune, *Doctors strike at Indian Hospitals to Protest Affirmative Action*, iht.com, 14-May-06.

586: Sandip Roy - Chowdhury, *Major US Companies are Setting Up Offices in India for Software Development. Is the Outsourcing of Jobs to India a Temporary Phenomenon?*, indiacurrents.com/news, 4-Aug-03.

587: Stephanie Crane, Tech Knowledge, *India's Outsourcers Gain Traction*, businessweek.com, 29-Oct-04.

592: TiE website, *TiE Website*, tie.org, Web Date 10/17/2006.

594: Grant Gross, IDG News Service, *Tech Worker Group Files Complaints Over H-1B Job Ads*, infoworld.com, 22-Jun-06.

597: BusinessWeek Online, *The Future of Technology: The Big Trends Ahead and Our Ranking of the Top 100 Info Tech Companies*, businessweek.com, 2005.

601: Wikipedia, *N.R. Narayana Murthy*, wikipedia.org/wiki, Web Date 4/15/2006.

602: VC Circle :: Early Stage/Angel, *Kanwal Rekhi Raising $150-$175 Million India-specific Fund*, vccircle.com/blog/EarlyStageAngel, 13-Feb-06.

603: Rep Tom Tancredo, *Representative Tom Tancredo's Speech Before the House of Representatives July 13, 2003*, american-champions.org/Presentations, 13-Jul-03.

604: Kim Gerard, *TiE -- The Secrets of Success*, tie-asia.org/events, Web Date 11/1/2005.

611: *There are Three Types of Student Visas*, going2usa.com/education/studentvisa.html, Web Date 2/28/2007.

612: *Exchange Visitor (J) Visas*, travel.state.gov/visa/temp/types, 28-Feb-07.

613: *ECFMG J-1 Visa Sponsorship Fact Sheet*, ecfmg.org/evsp/j1fact.html, 24-Sep-04.

615: Ron Schneiderman, Contributing Editor, *Offshoring. Outsourcing. Out of Work.*, Electronic Design, 20-Oct-05.

618: Wikipedia, *Non-Resident Indian and Person of Indian Origin*, en.wikipedia.org/wiki/Non-resident Indian and Person of Indian Origin, Web Date 3/9/2007.

619: Rick Merritt, *Where are the Programmers?*, Electronic Engineering Times, 12-Mar-07.

625: US India Political Action Committee, *USINPAC*, http://www.usinpac.com, Web Date 4/9/2007.

626: Josh Shaffer, Staff Writer, *A Little India, here in Raleigh*, The News and Observer, 29-Apr-07.

627: Christopher Reynolds, Los Angeles Times, *New Eyes on an Old Chinatown, San Francisco's miniature country offers wisdom still*, The News and Observer April 29, 2007, 29-Apr-07.

628: The News and Observer, *Duke Business School Hit by Cheating Scandal*, tmcnet.com, 30-Apr-07.

632: Vivek Wadhwa, Duke University, WRAL.com, *America's New Immigrant Entrepreneurs*, localtechwire.com/business, Web Date 5/3/2007.

634: Emily Flynn Vencat, Newsweek International, *Education: Why Everyone Cheats Now*, msnbc.msn.com/id/, 27-May-06.

635: Alan Finder, The New York Times, *34 Duke Business Students Face Discipline for Cheating*, www.nytimes.com, 1-May-07.

640: Show 321 Transcript, *Sizing Up the Competition*, foreignexchange.tv, 25-May-07.

644: Website, *Open Silicon Valley*, opensiliconvalley.com, Web Date 9/21/2007.

649: Wikipedia, *M.S. Krishnan*, wikipedia.org/wiki/M. S. Krishnan, 30-Dec-07.

653: *TiE has Helped Create Businesses Worth More than $200 Billion*, startinbusiness.co.us/flowchart/tie.htm, 1-Jan-00, Web Date 9/21/2007.

659: website, *About Tie*, tienewdelhi.org/members, Web Date 7/27/2007.

661: *IT Industry Finds Little to Like in Immigration Bill*, itbusinessedge.com, 31-May-07.

662: *Engineers Learning People Skills, Too*, att.net/, Web Date 12/9/2007.

665: *H-1B Visa*, wikipedia.org/wiki/H-1B visa, Web Date 1/2/2008.

666: Patrick Thibodeau, *H-1B Video Shocker: 'Our Goal is Clearly not to Find a Qualified? U.S. Worker'*, computerworld.com, 19-Jun-07.

670: Posted by Ann All December 10, 2007, *Boeing Is Latest Company to Learn Importance of Outsourcing Management*, itbusinessedge.com, 10-Dec-07.

682: Vikas Bajaj and Louise Story, *Mortgage Crisis Spreads Past Subprime Loans*, nytimes.com, 12-Feb-08.

685: Francis C. Assisi, *Skilled Indian Immigrants Create Wealth for America*, indolink.com, 4-Jan-07.

686: Who's Who of Asian Americans, *Who's Who of Asian Americans: Biography of Vivek Wadhwa*, asianamerica.net, Web Date 4/5/2008.

687: Vivek Wadhwa, Duke University, *Open Doors Wider for Skilled Immigrants*, businessweek.com, 3-Jan-07.

688: Ela Dutt, *Indian Owns a Goldmine*, tribuneindia.com, 16-May-08.

689: Gary Weiss, *Are You Paying for Corporate Fat Cats*, Parade, 13-Apr-08.

690: David Jackson, *McCain Denounces 'Siren Song' of Protectionism*, usatoday.com, 22-Apr-08.

693: Peggy Lim, *Fury Vented on Duke Student*, The News & Observer, 27-Apr-08.

696: *McKinsey & Company - Wikipedia, the free encyclopedia*, en.wikipedia.org, Web Date 5/14/2008.

703: Sheila Riley, *Green-card Red Tape Sends Valuable Engineers Packing*, eeTimes, 27-Aug-07.

709: Suzanne Gamboa, Associated Press Writer, *Labor Dept. Probes Work of Major Immigration Law Firm*, usatoday.com, 24-Jun-08.

716: andhra-pradesh-news, *Hyderabad Police Arrest 25 Foreign Students for Overstaying*, newkerala.com, 22-Oct-08.

719: Rhys Blakely in Bombay, *Madoff Tipster Blasts SEC, Says He Feared for His Safety*, foxnews.com, 4-Feb-09.

720: Tony Brown, *Why Indian H-1Bs Are Not Superior And Aframericans Are Not Cry Babies*, zazona.com, 7-Sep-01.

721: Manjeet Kripalani in Bombay, *Private Equity Pours Into India*, businessweek.com, 20-Jun-05.

724: *Syntel*, wikipedia.org, Web Date 8/9/2008.

725: *Mastech*, igatemastech.com, Web Date 8/9/2008.

726: Mary Beth Marklein, *U.S. School's Foreign Enrollments Soar*, usatoday.com, 16-Nov-08.

727: Grant Gross, IDG News Service, *Foreign Students Get Longer U.S. Stay*, pcworld.com, 12-Apr-08.

728: Hadley Gambie, *As Economy Slumps, Firms Line Up to Hire Skilled Foreign Workers*, foxnews.com, 19-Mar-09.

730: Patrick Thibodeau, *H-1B, Offshoring Supporters Get Key Obama Administration Posts*, computerworld.com, 3-Feb-09.

731: Patrick Thibodeau, *Why Obama May Back the H-1B Increase Even In a Recession*, computerworld.com, 6-Nov-08.

732: *New Jobless Claims Jump Unexpectedly to 669,000*, foxnews.com, 2-Apr-09.

733: Susan Page, *24 Million Go From 'Thriving' to 'Struggling'*, usatoday.com, 9-Mar-09.

735: Lalit K Jha in Washington, *H-1B: Indian CEOs Meet Obama Team*, business.rediff.com, 19-Mar-09.

737: Associated Press, *Lawmakers Prosper Despite Economic Slump*, usatoday.com, 16-Jun-08.

741: Marianne Kolbasuk McGee, *Should H-1B Employers Pay for US Students' Degrees*, informationweek.com/blog, 1-Nov-06.

742: Vivek Wadhwa, TechCrunch blog, *Free the H-1Bs, Free the Economy*, techcrunch.com, 30-Aug-09.

743: Christian Dugas, USA Today, *College Graduates Struggle to Repay Student Loans*, usatoday.com, 12-May-09.

744: Emily Bazar, USA Today, *More of the World's Talented Workers Opt to Leave USA*, usatoday.com, 20-Sep-09.

745: Dr. Norman Matloff, *Globalization and the American IT Worker*, Communications of the ACM, 1-Nov-04.

746: Dr. Norman Matloff, *Offshoring What Can Go Wrong?*, IT Pro, 1-Jul-05.

753: The Associated Press, *Supreme Court Turns Down Appeal From InfoSpace Founder*, seattletimesnwsource.com, 9-Mar-09.

754: *US Embassy Alerts Cops on Fake Student Visa Rackets*, telugudreams.com/News/NewsDetails, 17-Jan-10.

755: Stephen Labaton, *S.E.C.'s Embattled Chief Resigns in Wake of Latest Political Storm*, nytimes.com, 6-Nov-02.

756: Associated Press, *Settlement is Approved in Qwest Lawsuit*, Salt Lake City, Desert News, 30-Sep-06.

766: Peter S. Goodman, Washington Post, *How China is Making the Pen as Mighty as the PC*, umsl.edu, 12-Dec-02.

770: Eryn Brown and David Kirkpatrick, Fortune, *The Reverse Brain Drain*, umsl.edu, 11-Nov-02.

774: Paula Musich, eWeek, *Offshore Upstarts*, umsl.edu, 23-Sep-02.

776: Knowledg@Wharton, *The Case For and Against, Shifting Back-Office Operations Overseas*, umsl.edu, 9-Oct-02.

778: Jack Anderson and Douglas Cohn, *SEC Needs New Leader*, ljworld.com, 20-Jul-02.

779: *Testimony of Vivek Wadhwa To the U.S. House of Representatives Committee on Education and the Workforce*, , 16-May-06.

780: Professor Norm Matloff's H-1B Web Page, *The H-1B is Fundamentally about Cheap Labor*, heather.cs.ucdavis.edu, Web Date 1/18/2010.

840: Associated Press, *Bill Clinton's Foreign Affairs May Cost Clinton Chance of Secretary of State*, elections.foxnews.com, 15-Nov-08.

915: Henry Unger, *Student Loan Debt is Now More than Credit Card Debt*, The Biz Beat, 12-Apr-11.

923: Ted C. Fishman, *Why the Jobs are Going Over There*, usatoday.com, 17-May-11.

924: Adam Shell, USA Today, *Hedge Fund Manager Rajaratnam Guilt in Insider Trading Trial*, usatoday.com, 11-May-11.

927: Valerie Richardson, The Washington Times, *House Members in the Know Score 'Abnormal' Stock Profits, Study Says*, washingtontimes.com, 25-May-11.

949: John Miano, *When in Doubt, Make It Up*, cis.org, 23-Aug-11.

966: Julianne Pepitone, *Tech Job Cuts Hit 4-Year High*, money.cnn.com, 19-Jan-10.

967: Open Doors, Institute of International Education, *International Student Enrollments Rose Modestly in 2009/10, Led by Stron Increase in Students From China*, iie.org, 15-Nov-10.

968: Voice of IT Management, *End of the Era of Mega Outsourcing Deals*, computerworldus.com, 10-Apr-10.

969: *508 Outsourcing Deals Signed in Q1 2011: Report*, economictimes.indiatimes.com.

970: Bureau of Labor Statistics, *Bankrupting America A Project of Public Notice*, bls.gov/cps/tables.htm, 3-Jun-11.

971: Sarah Anderson, chuck Collins, Scott Klinger, Sam Pizzigati, *Executive Excess 2011: The Massive CEO Rewards for Tax Dodging*, ips-dc.org, 31-Aug-11.

972: Jim Tankersley, *The Phantom 15 Million*, nationaljournal.com, 21-Jan-11.

974: Project Vote Smart, *HR 3012- Repeals Certain Green Card Limitations*, votesmart.org, 5-Jan-12.

978: Julia Preston, The New York Times, *Easier Route to Green Card to be Proposed for Some*, nytimes.com, 7-Jan-12.

980: Institute of International Education, Inc, *International Student Enrollments Increased by 5 Percent in 2010/11, Led by Strong Increase in Students from China*, iie.org/en, Web Date 1/12/2012.

983: *Chinese Applicants to U.S. Schools Skyrocket.*, patriotupdate.com, 12-Jan-12.

985: Danielle Kurtzleben, *10 States With the Largest Budget Shortfalls*, usnews.com/news/articles, 14-Jan-11.

1017: Tom Lauricella, *Since End of 1999, U.S. Stocks Performance Has Been the All-Time Clunker; Even 1930's Beat It*, wsj.com, 20-Dec-09.

1018: *Rajat Gupta's Trial Enters Second Week, Early Edge for US Prosecutors?*, ndtv.com, 29-May-12.

1019: Schumpter, *The Rajat Gupta Trial, The Bad-Bushel Defense*, economist.com, 30-May-12.

1020: Wayne Allyn Root, *The Scandal at Columbia that Ends the Obama Presidency: ROOT for America@*, posted by personalliberty on YouTube, 14-Aug-12.

1021: William M. Fish, President of the Washington International Education Council, *Getting Your Student Visa*, studyusa.com/en/a/ee/getting-your-student-visa, Web Date 10/31/2012.

1039: Associated Press, *1.9 Million 2011 Foreclosures are Fewest Since 2007*, usatoday.com, 12-Jan-12.

1066: Allan Dodds Frank, *Rajat Gupta Was Found Guilty of Insider trading in Less Than a Day*, thedailybeast.com, 15-Jun-12.

Index

What We Need to Do to Protect Our Economic Competitiveness and National Security.

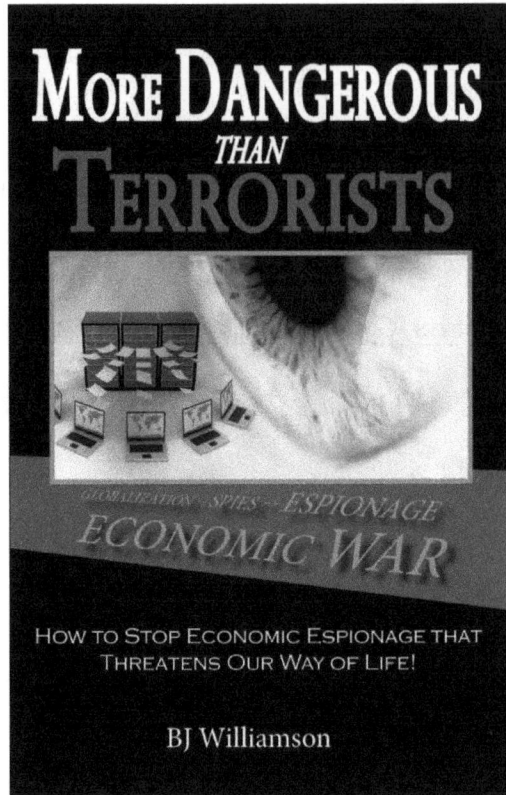

Discover how outsourcing enables espionage, and fuels trade deficits that let foreign countries acquire US businesses threatening our national security and way of life. Outsourcing has also secretly been used to fund building foreign military threats.

To order: **More Dangerous than Terrorists**

go to: *Amazon.com*

Or to learn more go to: *www.lanitepublishing.com*

What We Need to Do to Take Back Our Country.

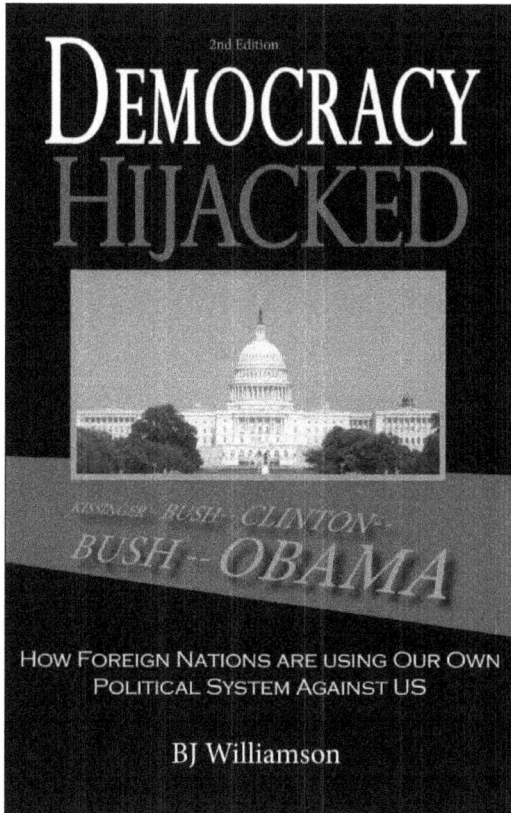

Discover how foreign nations are using money to manipulate our elections, and how corporate executives are recruited to become lobbyists to get legislation passed that enables transferring our jobs to foreign workers using visas and offshoring.

To order: **Democracy Hijacked**

Go to: *Amazon.com*

Or to learn more go to: *www.lanitepublishing.com*

www.ingramcontent.com/pod-product-compliance
Lightning Source LLC
Chambersburg PA
CBHW060555200326
41521CB00007B/574